MW00653213

THE SEXUALLY SATISFIED WOMAN

The Sexually Satisfied Woman

The 5-Step Program for Getting Everything You Want in Bed

Dr. Ronnie Edell

A DUTTON BOOK

DUTTON
Published by the Penguin Group
Penguin Books USA Inc., 375 Hudson Street,
New York, New York 10014, U.S.A.
Penguin Books Ltd, 27 Wrights Lane, London W8 5TZ, England
Penguin Books Australia Ltd, Ringwood, Victoria, Australia
Penguin Books Canada Ltd, 10 Alcorn Avenue,
Toronto, Ontario, Canada M4V 3B2
Penguin Books (N.Z.) Ltd, 182–190 Wairau Road,
Auckland 10, New Zealand

Penguin Books Ltd, Registered Offices:
Harmondsworth, Middlesex, England

First published by Dutton, an imprint of Dutton Signet,
a division of Penguin Books USA Inc.
Distributed in Canada by McClelland & Stewart Inc.

First Printing, October, 1994
10 9 8 7 6 5 4 3 2

LIBRARY OF CONGRESS CATALOGING IN PUBLICATION DATA
Edell, Ronnie.
    The sexually satisfied woman : the 5-step program for getting
everything you want in bed / Ronnie Edell.
        p.   cm.
    ISBN 0-525-93677-7
    1. Sex instruction for women. 2. Women—Sexual behavior.
3. Self-help techniques.   I. Title.
HQ46.E33   1994
613.9'6—dc20   94-9573
                                                        CIP

Printed in the United States of America
Set in Goudy Old Style

To every woman who ever believed that sex could be something more than it is. Your natural inner creativity can set you free in the bedroom and give you all the pleasure you deserve. I hope this book will help you find that pleasure and the happiness in your relationship that it can bring.

ACKNOWLEDGMENTS

~

A book is a collaborative effort, and although one person's name is inevitably on the cover, an army of people struggle in the background to endure the joys and pains of bringing a project such as this into reality. Just as many people share in the creation of a movie, here is where we "roll the credits" for this book.

I'd like to thank my agent, Michael Hamilburg, who is a gentleman and a genius in his chosen field of endeavor, as well as a very special friend. It is testament to Michael's business acumen that he was able to see the potential for the future in this project. Thanks too to his associate, Joanie Socola, who has always been there with a kind word and wise advice, and no small measure of savvy of her own.

I'd like to thank Michaela Hamilton, my editor at NAL/Dutton, who had the foresight to take this project on and nurture it through the "birthing" stages. She too had the vision to see what could be, and has been an incredible guide through this journey, providing me tre-

Dr. Ronnie Edell

mendous insights, and the benefit of her expertise every step of the way. It is only through her tenacious efforts that this book has become a reality and has come into being. Thanks too to her associate Jennifer Enderlin, who offered valuable comments on the manuscript, and whose insights helped shape this book in its current form.

A special thank-you to the entire Viking/Penguin "family." I have felt nothing but warmth and friendship, and a sense of belonging in this family from the beginning of this project. A very special thank-you to Elaine Koster of NAL/Dutton for her belief in this book, and her tenacity in bringing the project into the fold. I owe her a debt of gratitude that is more than she may know.

An extra special thanks to my good friend Barbara Lagowski, whose editorial wizardry helped transform a fundamentally good but weighty manuscript into a slim, streamlined, bestselling page turner that goes beyond "kiss and tell."

Thank you to my wife, Barbara, love of my life, who has stood by me through thick and thin, and been a companion to me in all that I do. Thanks also to Lillian and Edward Bomes, my in-laws, for having given me the greatest gift of my life: Barbara.

To our two beautiful daughters, Ricki and Sherri, who have given me the twinkle in each eye and have given us both much joy. They have grown proud and strong, and it is a pleasure to see them become young adults.

A big kiss to our three Samoyeds, Teddy, Christy, and Sammy—the three bears—who have given our family lots of hugs, love, and joy.

A very special thank-you to my parents, Philip and Florence, for their love, support, strength, guidance, understanding, and belief in me over all these years. Dad and Mom, the freedom to achieve that you have given your children, and the happiness that you have allowed them to experience, goes beyond anything one can expect from two parents. Thank you and I love you.

I feel a special sense of gratitude to my clients and those who attended my seminars, all of whom were willing to face their fears and inhibitions about sex to move beyond them into a place where they could achieve happiness, contentment, and pleasure both within themselves and within their relationships.

Finally, I want to thank all the people who read and commented on the manuscript in its various stages, for giving their time and energy and offering their insights and advice. It has made the book a better vehicle for communicating the message that sex can be fun.

CONTENTS

~

~

Introduction: Getting the Satisfaction You Want From the Man You Love

~

Some months ago, when this book was still in the writing stages, I ran into an acquaintance at a party. When she asked what I had been up to, I told her that I was working on a manuscript based on some workshops and seminars I'd been conducting. The name of my book would be *The Sexually Satisfied Woman*.

"The sexually satisfied woman? Ha!" she said, loudly enough to attract the attention of everyone in the room. "Well, let me know when you find one. *If* you find one."

Are erotically blissed-out, physically satisfied women really harder to find than the mythical G spot? Are most women—particularly those committed to long-term partnerships or marriages—silently frustrated by otherwise good relationships that offer stability rather than stimulation? Routine sexual activity rather than unrestrained sexual fulfillment? Unfortunately, they are.

According to a recent poll of thousands of married women, a full 67 percent said they were not getting enough sex. In another poll of more than a thousand women, only 23 percent said they had "no complaints" about the way their partners treated them in bed. The remainder of these women yearned for their partners to be more sensitive, to pay attention to their needs, slow down, last longer, show more intimacy, be more spontaneous, improve their technique, or be willing to experiment sexually. In yet another poll of nearly fourteen hundred women, a whopping 91 percent said that there was still a double standard in sex—that men get to have all the fun. What all these statistics boil down to is that sexual boredom is a major source of frustration or marital friction. And since boredom in the bedroom breeds a litany of related complaints—infrequent sex, sex without orgasm, "mechanical" orgasm with no real excitement—more women than ever are finding it difficult to get complete satisfaction—wild, passionate, can't-get-enough satisfaction—with the men they love.

If you are sexually dissatisfied, unfulfilled, or wanting in any way, rest assured you are not alone. In my twenty years of private practice helping women, men, and couples in areas such as intimacy, marriage, relationships, infidelity, and love, no topic has generated more heat among my female clients than sexual frustration. Of course, sex is a shared experience—and men *do* get their share of disappointment and monotony. But while men are conditioned to take control of their sex lives, even encouraged to seek satisfaction wherever their adventuring penises might lead them, women have been socialized to deny their natural needs and desires. Generations of "good girls" have been brought up to believe that it is not healthy to be too aware of sexual feelings, that it is not acceptable to reveal or even *have* sexual fantasies, and that when it comes to acting on their natural desires, well ... good girls just *don't*. Can it really surprise us that so many women end up in a sexual rut? They've been given the means to bury their passion and submerge their needs and none of the tools to climb back out!

Fortunately, there is a way out of unfulfilled and unfulfilling sex. And its success doesn't depend on weeks of monotonous exercises, your partner's consent, or even your partner's knowledge. In fact, all it takes to discover the sexually satisfied woman within you is the desire to fulfill your most exciting erotic fantasies—and the willingness to express every facet of your boundless sexual nature.

Getting Yours. This is a powerful book. It is a book that puts the explosive energy of sex directly into your hands. And it is an uplifting book. It will boost your self-confidence, elevate your ability to give and receive pleasure, and lift your spirits sexually.

Perhaps you think your sex life is fine for now. If you are enjoying regular orgasms and you and your lover are content with the way things are, that may be so. Still, I'd like to suggest that your erotic encounters can reward you with much more than mere contentment and "regular" orgasm. Based on your own deepest desires, fed by your vast resources of sexual energy, the techniques you will learn in this book will kindle a spectacular sensual awakening, making each sexual encounter electric, arousing, and exhilarating beyond your wildest dreams.

If you are sexually bored, dissatisfied, frustrated or discontented in any way, this book was written with you—and your total gratification—in mind. Within days (maybe hours!) after reading this book, you will be tapping into your most pleasurable fantasies to add newness, intrigue, and sparkle to your sex life. Within weeks, those fantasies—and every sexual encounter— will come alive, more powerfully and memorably than you could ever have imagined.

If lovemaking with your partner has stalled, even if the tank of passion that fueled your relationship seems to have run completely dry, the techniques you discover in this book are certain to jump-start your ongoing af- fair with your spouse or lover. You will teach your part- ner how to turn you on in a way you've never been turned on before, to touch you exactly the way you want to be touched, at the precise moment that brings you to ecstasy. Most of all, because my Five-Step Pro- gram focuses entirely on *your* complete fulfillment, this book shows you how to bring out the "savage" in any man, to get him to satisfy your wildest desires, to get and keep the upper hand in bed, so you can create the ultimate in sexual pleasure first for yourself, *then* for your lover.

Of course, no sexual encounter—not even a mind- blowing, spine-tingling sensual blitz—can alleviate long-term or deep-seated marital difficulties. Still, in the ten years since I first introduced my Five-Step Sex- ual Satisfaction Training Program, the response from women has been so positive I've included a sampling here:

- My sexual pleasure increased, and so did my desire for sex.

- For the first time, I feel good about myself sexu- ally.

- Sex is fun, exciting, passionate, and spontaneous again.

- Now the way I make love, and the length of time I make love, is entirely up to me. Am I more satisfied? You bet!

- This program has put the adventure and intrigue back into sex.

- I've always enjoyed having fantasies, but now that I'm living them out ... well, let's just say real is better.

- Bigger orgasms and more of them. That's what I got out of this program.

- Asking for what I wanted in bed not only got me what I wanted in bed, it made me more confident in other areas of my life, too.

- I was able to get my partner so turned on, he was willing to do anything I asked. I loved it! And so did he.

- The biggest surprise is that I actually feel younger. In fact, my husband and I are like young lovers again. We're more intimate, more playful ... we're even holding hands in public!

Does the Sexually Satisfied Woman Really Exist? As I told the skeptical friend who challenged me at the party, you can bet your last garter belt she does! The potential to become an unrestrained, totally gratified sexual adventurer is within the reach of every woman who wants to throw off the shackles of her inhibitions.

Look into the passionate heart of your own desire and you have found her.

From the LoveSkills Makeover and PowerTease Method to the highly charged play-acting techniques, the simple, pleasurable lessons in this book have already transformed the sex lives of hundreds of women. Use them to reclaim the sexual energy that is naturally yours and you'll become a dynamo, grabbing for all the erotic gusto you can, riding every sexual experience to heights you never imagined.

In short, you will become the totally fulfilled woman you know you can be. And your adventures between the sheets will never be routine again.

1 ~

Has It Been Good for You, Darling? Take the Sexual Satisfaction Quiz

~

"The honeymoon is over." "As soon as you say, 'I do,' you don't anymore." "When the ring goes on, the libido goes off." "Sleep together long enough and know what you'll get? Very well rested." If people could express their erotic desires as creatively as they do their sexual boredom, there would be no sexual boredom to express!

Of course, some of these one-liners *are* funny. They can even help you to laugh off any temporary dry spells you might experience in the course of your relationship. But if zingers like "love dies—passion goes on life support" have made their way into popular stand-up routines, it's because sex has become infrequent, dull and routine for too many couples. And for the thousands of women whose fantasies have become more vivid and dynamic than their sex lives, that's no laughing matter.

Perhaps you've been sleeping with the man you love—but you're more well-rested than you'd like. Maybe you're wondering why your physical encounters aren't as dazzling, arousing and memorable as your fantasies. Perhaps the wham-bam pattern you've fallen into between the sheets is causing you to fall out of lust with your partner. To you I say, there's only one thing worth losing sleep over . . . and it certainly isn't *lackluster* sex!

The truth is, it really doesn't matter which symptom of sexual dissatisfaction prompted you to pick up this book. It doesn't even matter if the reason for your unhappiness is something you (or your lover) can't seem to put your finger on. Simply by selecting this book, you opted to begin an adventure that will reenergize your libido, revive your sensuality, and take you to the ultimate fulfillment of your limitless sexual destiny. And while it is a journey like none other, it begins as all journeys do—by pinpointing where you are now.

My Sexual Satisfaction Quiz is a time-tested instrument for measuring the level of satisfaction you are currently getting from your marriage or relationship. Developed over years of research and based on the experiences of hundreds of women just like you, it will help you assess your assertiveness in bed, understand your inhibitions, and decide if the sex you're getting is the kind of sex you want. It will help you heighten your awareness of sexual boundaries between you and your partner, gauge your ability to express your physical needs, and, ultimately, create in your own life all the thrilling sexual encounters that live in your imagination.

Has sex been good for you? It should take you only a few minutes to find out. Read each item carefully, then choose the response that most accurately reflects your situation. Answer all the questions, and be as truthful as you can. Remember: sex is an experience we all come to naked, so don't be put off by questions that require baring all. An investment in honesty now will pay big dividends later.

If you can't decide between two numbers, circle the lower one—this will give you more of an opportunity to improve. If you're in doubt on any question, make your best guess, but be sure to answer all of them. When you're finished, add up your answers and refer to the scoring chart that follows.

DR. RONNIE EDELL'S
SEXUAL SATISFACTION QUIZ

1. When I think about my partner, I get turned on.

    4 Always or almost always
    3 Most of the time
    2 About half the time
    1 Some of the time
    0 Hardly ever or never

2. I look forward to our lovemaking encounters.

    4 Always or almost always
    3 Most of the time
    2 About half the time
    1 Some of the time
    0 Hardly ever or never

3. I initiate sex:

    4 At least as often as my partner
    3 Less than he does, but reasonably often
    2 Sometimes, but much less than he does

    1 Very rarely
    0 Almost never or never

[Note: If you initiate substantially more often than your partner but feel frustrated by that, score according to how often *your partner* initiates sex: for example, 1 if he rarely initiates sex, 0 if he never does.]

4. Sex with my partner is exciting. When we make love, sparks fly.

    4 Always or almost always
    3 Most of the time
    2 About half the time
    1 Some of the time
    0 Hardly ever or never

5. When my partner and I make love, we try new positions and techniques.

    4 Always or almost always
    3 Most of the time
    2 About half the time
    1 Some of the time
    0 Hardly ever or never

6. I am assertive in bed. I take an active role in getting the pleasure I want.

    4 Always or almost always
    3 Most of the time
    2 About half the time
    1 Some of the time
    0 Hardly ever or never

7. I am honest with my partner in bed. If what we're doing is not enjoyable, I let him know rather than pretend to enjoy it.

    4   Always or almost always
    3   Most of the time
    2   About half the time
    1   Some of the time
    0   Hardly ever or never

[Note: If you fake orgasms in bed, answer this question according to how often you do so. 4: never or hardly ever; 3: occasionally; 2: moderately often; 1: very often; 0: at every or nearly every lovemaking session.]

8. Although I am open to experimentation and try to accommodate my partner where possible, if he wants me to do something unpleasurable in bed, I try to negotiate a compromise rather than force myself to do it.

    4   Always or almost always
    3   Most of the time
    2   About half the time
    1   Some of the time
    0   Hardly ever or never

9. My partner touches me in exactly the right places and exactly the right ways to satisfy me.

    4   Always or almost always
    3   Most of the time
    2   About half the time
    1   Some of the time
    0   Hardly ever or never

10. When I make love with my partner, my mind is focused on what we are doing, not wandering off into thoughts of other men or chores I have to do.

    4   Always or almost always
    3   Most of the time
    2   About half the time
    1   Some of the time
    0   Hardly ever or never

11. I talk in bed. I express my pleasure and ask for what I want, even using sexy language when I feel like it.

    4   Always or almost always
    3   Most of the time
    2   About half the time
    1   Some of the time
    0   Hardly ever or never

12. I tease my partner, making him wait a little bit for his gratification, rather than giving him everything he wants right away.

    4   Always or almost always
    3   Most of the time
    2   About half the time
    1   Some of the time
    0   Hardly ever or never

13. I talk about my sexual fantasies during lovemaking to turn both of us on.

    4   Always or almost always
    3   Most of the time
    2   About half the time

1   Some of the time
0   Hardly ever or never

14. If I want to act out one of my sexual fantasies with my partner, such as making love in another part of the house, dressing up and playing a role, or trying a completely new sexual activity, I go ahead and do it.

    4   Always or almost always
    3   Most of the time
    2   About half the time
    1   Some of the time
    0   Hardly ever or never

15. Based on the sex life I share with my partner, I would say that the chances of my marriage or relationship being threatened by infidelity are:

    4   Slim to none
    3   Very unlikely
    2   Possible
    1   Likely, possibly happening right now
    0   Certain, or definitely happening right now

Now add up your score for the fifteen questions and check it against the chart that follows.

46–60   Congratulations! You have taught your lover what it takes to satisfy you. And who knows? You may even be able to teach us all a thing or two!

Your answers make it apparent that sex is an important resource to you, you know how to please yourself, and you enjoy an exceptionally satisfying sex life. And since you are active, assertive, and creative in the bedroom, your partner is probably just as satisfied (and exhausted!) as you are.

If I know you, you will read this book from cover to cover, just to be sure you aren't missing any techniques that could make your relationship even more exciting and fulfilling. Enjoy—and carry on! You are a rare individual who has achieved a rare level of fulfillment.

31–45   You have a good sex life, but it could be better. I know you can jump to the next scoring level by the end of this book, and I encourage you, as you go through the book, to work on those areas that are holding you back from the ultimate enjoyment of sex.

You are not as assertive in bed as you can be, and you are giving in to your sexual fears and inhibitions to some degree. Perhaps you are trying too hard to please your partner without giving your own needs priority; or you are holding back from sharing your sexual desires with him. You may even be giving him too many unjustified compliments to soothe his ego, at the expense of your own pleasure.

Although you've got a better-than-average sex life, I think you sense that something is holding you back from being as open as you can be sexually. Because this book is all about dispelling the inhibitions that lead to sexual frustration, I know my Five-Step Program can put you over the top—in more ways than one!

And once you get into the top scoring range, you'll have better things to do than keep score!

16–30   Because most people score within this range, it's fair to say that you have an average sex life. Of course, that doesn't mean that you don't experience erotic peaks. You do. But your passivity, inhibitions, and willingness to "go with the flow" makes achieving those sexual highs a hit or miss proposition.

Of all the scoring groups, you are in perhaps the most interesting position. To describe it metaphorically, you are perched gamely on a fence, with your unfulfilled sexual desires on one side and your willingness to accept the status quo on the other. At times, your underlying desire to liberate your sexuality may be strong enough to make you teeter momentarily, but your fear of revealing your true sexual self is stronger. You always return to the safety of middle ground.

But is your position really safe? You're definitely not getting what you want. You may even be faking orgasm—and that kind of frustration engenders a litany of problems in a relationship. You've settled into a pattern of sexual monotony that parallels most people's work lives, so sex probably isn't fun and games for your partner, either. As for those private fantasies you substitute for real satisfaction? Watch it. They could push you—or your partner—into an affair.

You know that sex *can* be a powerful, even

explosive, experience if you can just put the fireworks back into your love life. Don't settle for bedroom burnout! With a little motivation and the help of this book, you can turn your private fantasies into a fabulous playground for two, take your relationship from mundane to magnificent, and make the sparks fly!

0–15 Welcome to the real world. You'd be surprised how many people score in this range. Take heart that you're not alone and remember: this book was written for you.

On the up side, you have more opportunity to improve than anyone who has taken this quiz. And because your answers reflect both honesty and motivation, I know you have what it takes to change your self-defeating attitudes, take charge of your sensual needs, and make the leap from sexual frustration to total satisfaction.

For now, though, your sex life is clearly not going to propel you to the heights of passion. You are a classic "pleaser": you probably have sex more often to fulfill the obligations of your relationship than to gratify your own needs. Self-sacrificing to a fault, you may also be faking orgasm regularly, a ploy that fuels your partner's ego while telling your own to "hit the road." Needless to say, you are not getting much enjoyment out of sex, nor are you likely to unless you stop waiting for pleasure to find you and begin taking it for yourself.

If you have quietly tucked your sexual self away like some priceless antique, take cover:

the family jewels are about to burst out of the closet! And if you feel that you have lost touch with your sensuality, your desire, or your partner, hang on: this book will open a direct line to ecstasy—one that will lead you to a closer, happier bond with the man you love.

The Quiz: It's Not Just Another One-Night Stand. Sexuality isn't a one-shot deal—and neither is this quiz! Of course, you must begin the Five-Step Program by taking the Sexual Satisfaction Quiz. The clearer your understanding of your current sexual happiness, the clearer your path to ecstasy will be.

But the fulfillment of sexuality is an ongoing process, and I encourage you to take the Sexual Satisfaction Quiz periodically to monitor your improvement as you work through this book. The women who have taken my seminars have found that quarterly or semiannual "tune-ups" keep them on the path of sexual fulfillment. I suggest you mark your calendar for one month from the day you begin the program and retake the quiz then. (The results will surprise and motivate you!) Finally, to keep yourself from slipping back into negative habits (like faking orgasms or not asking for what you want), take it once a month for the next six months and beyond that, at half-year intervals, or as you see fit. A great sex life is a consistent sex life—and longevity takes stamina. Getting some positive feedback from the quiz will help you to hang in there for the good stuff.

When you feel brave enough, you may even want to have your partner take the Sexual Satisfaction Quiz. Many women report that comparing answers with a lover has led to greater sexual intimacy—and hearing from your significant other could lead to a significantly happier bond for you.

It's Your Turn. The Sexual Satisfaction Quiz strikes deep. It is bound to reveal some unfulfilled needs that may be frustrating your mate. As you discuss his answers, his desires, or even his demands, it's important to remind yourself that the purpose of this program is to make each sexual experience more pleasurable for *you.*

Isn't that selfish? No! Unless you make your needs a priority in your mind, your gratification will never become a priority in your bed! Besides, sexual enthusiasm is contagious. While you're grabbing all the erotic gusto you can get, you are also grabbing your man in the most powerful erogenous zone of all: the imagination. Take hold of him where it counts, and his heart, his mind, and your mutual happiness will surely follow.

To put the guiding principle underlying this book another way: "If mama ain't happy, ain't nobody happy!" And ain't it the truth! If the women who have made my Five-Step Program an active part of their lovemaking have given me enough testimonials to fill a book, the positive feedback I've gotten from their lucky partners could fill a second volume! Of course, sexual satisfaction is very much a "different strokes for different folks" proposition; each of these couples is blissfully living out the fantasies that are unique to them. Still, the bottom-line benefits that have reenergized their sex lives can certainly rev up yours. Within weeks, you can expect that. . .

- Sex will become more fun, playful and exciting than you've ever dreamed possible. You'll tease the way you did when your relationship was new, laugh from unbridled pleasure, maybe wrestle a little . . . and lock monotony out of your bedroom forever.

- You'll become a sexual adventurer. Like an intrepid explorer, you'll seek out thrilling new positions, tantalizing new techniques, and countless new places to stimulate your adventurous spirit. And because sex will be an ongoing quest for you, you'll never make love in the same way twice!

- The frequency of your lovemaking will dramatically increase. Full of passionate fire, you'll find yourself making love as often as four or five times a week . . . or even several times a day!

- You'll extend the length of your lovemaking sessions. The powerful teasing techniques you will learn in this book will enable you to keep your partner on the brink of orgasm *for hours,* while you take the time and pleasure you need to satisfy yourself.

- You'll be the tiger in bed you were meant to be, initiating the sexual experience you want, at the moment you want it most.

- You'll turn the man you love into the lover of your dreams. Because this program puts you—and your partner—in touch with your body's hot spots, he'll learn to stroke you the way you want to be stroked, follow your lead to heights of passion, and please you every time you make love. And most of all:

- You'll bring to life all of the thrilling sexual encounters that exist in your wildest fantasies. The fact that you experience sexual fantasies (and we all do!) means you are more of an erotic inventor than you know. It also means you are closer to getting everything you want in bed than you think.

As you will understand more fully in the next chapter, your sexual fantasies aren't just passing fancies. They are vivid images of your very real feelings; manifestations of your most intimate desires; explicit broadcasts of the techniques, positions, and scenarios that stimulate your mind and arouse your body to its core. Sexually speaking, they are reflections of your purest self—the liberated you who feels and expresses pleasure without inhibition, who pursues pleasure without embarrassment or shame. My Five-Step Program has but a single goal: to enable you to release the lusty, adventurous essence of your sexual self, first for your pleasure, then for your lover's. The process begins with an excursion to the source of all sexual satisfaction—a place I call the Well of Sexual Dreams.

2 ～

The Well of Sexual Dreams: Your Passport to Ultimate Sexual Pleasure

～

I'd like to tell you the story of Laura. Laura is a classic case, a "textbook" case, of a sexually dissatisfied woman struggling to find meaning in her intimate life and derive pleasure from her sexuality. Her story is a vivid illustration of the way women's sexuality is pushed underground by societal pressures. It is also a paean to those women who successfully free themselves of their sexual fears, overcome their inhibitions, and open themselves to the limitless pleasures of sexuality.

Laura, thirty-four years old, is married to Jim. Together with their two children, Laura and Jim form the typical two-career family of the 1990s.

Society Teaches Women Not to Enjoy Sex. Laura grew up in the '50s and early '60s, when dolls were molded without sexual organs and little girls were molded in the likeness of dolls. In her household sex was a four-letter word—and masturbation was a punishable offense. ("No! Don't do that! Don't touch yourself there.

It's dirty.") Even menstruation was cloaked in secrecy. Unable to approach such a sexually charged topic, Laura's parents never prepared her for the onset of her period. As a result, Laura came to view menstruation not as an important and natural rite of passage but as a trauma: something dirty, shameful, and unpleasant.

Laura's formal sex education began over her father's vigorous and public objections. However, he needn't have bothered petitioning the school board. In class, Laura was never taught that sex could be pleasurable. The curriculum was strictly sperm and egg stuff, with a smattering of frightening information about pregnancy and disease thrown in as a curiosity inhibitor. For Laura, sex was something that happened under a microscope—not between the sheets.

It wasn't until Laura reached college that she began to learn, from books and magazine articles, that her body could give her pleasure. But by then she faced the daunting task of undoing all her early indoctrination: that sex was an offense punishable by pregnancy or disease; that it was a subject nice girls didn't talk about, a pastime only "bad" girls indulged in.

When, in her thirties, Laura finally confronted her mother on her sexual silence, she was shocked to learn that repression had been handed down from generation to generation, from grandmother to mother to daughter, like a prized family heirloom. It took Laura a split second to decide that this hand-me-down was totally out of place in her modern marriage. But by then, her passivity was part of the household routine—even for her husband, Jim. In fact, it was Jim, Laura ultimately discovered, who unconsciously prevented her from being all she could be in bed.

Male Ambivalence Toward the Sexually Aggressive Woman. For as long as he could remember, Jim was taught that sex is a man's game: a competitive sport in which he could "letter" in virility. In high school Jim and his friends compared notes about the young women they had seduced. Later, in college, Jim actually began to keep score. It didn't matter that his hard and fast figures reduced his sexual partners to ciphers; to Jim it was a way to quantify his status as a man.

If marriage wasn't a route to instant sexual liberation for Laura, neither was a trip down the aisle a transformational experience for Jim. To him, marital relations were the Super Bowl of sex. The bedroom was the home field where, if luck was with him, he would call the shots, complete his passes, and dash (a bit too quickly for Laura's satisfaction) into the end zone. Laura was merely a cheerleader in his game to prove himself. It never occurred to Jim that she was entitled to have a game plan of her own.

The few times Laura tried to take the upper hand in bed, or position herself so that sex would be stimulating for her, she was rebuffed by Jim. Make no mistake: Jim *wanted* Laura to have pleasure in bed. Her orgasms were proof that he had "scored"—but the touchdowns only counted if he had been able to please his wife on *his* terms. Each time Laura struggled to take her own pleasure in bed, Jim felt in danger of losing his superior position. If Laura managed to please herself, what would his role be in her erotic life? What could any man be if not a star performer in his own bed? An emasculated wimp? The sexual equal of a *woman?*

Faced with deep and discomfiting questions like these, a man's man can do only one thing: minimize his discomfort. And Jim did just that. To bypass his feelings and protect his masculinity, Jim immersed himself in machismo. He began to exercise tighter control over Laura. When necessary, he physically overpowered her to keep her from engineering her own pleasure. Laura, meanwhile, found a more creative outlet for her frustrated urges: the Well of Sexual Dreams.

The Well of Sexual Dreams. Unexpressed sexual feelings do not go away; they go into long-term storage. And so it was with Laura's stifled erotic impulses.

Early in her marriage, while making love to Jim, Laura would experience deep inner stirrings that were just out of reach of her conscious awareness. One night, she felt a haunting impulse to shout out her secret sexual longings loud enough for the neighbors to hear; during another tryst, she experienced a fleeting urge to call Jim a naughty name then pin his hands down while she got on top of him, as if he were her hapless sexual slave. Since Laura knew that Jim would not be receptive to any physical expression of her deep sexual needs, Laura carefully buried her cravings, certain that these feelings would never be heard from again. But her frustrated desires did recur—often and vividly—in the form of graphic and arousing fantasies.

Over the years, however, Laura learned to submerge her fantasies the same way that she did her physical desires. Often, she wasn't even aware of them. But some of the fantasies were very intense. When these vivid reflections of her thwarted sexuality played themselves out like erotic films projected by her mind, Laura couldn't help but acknowledge her powerful longings. Nor could she avoid noticing that her sexual dreams had taken on specific themes, each representing a sexual impulse that had been denied:

- She wanted Jim to "use" her as his sexual play-thing and make love to her passionately and forcefully.

- She wanted to experience sex with mirrors suspended in the bedroom so she could watch as she and Jim writhed passionately on the bed.

- She wanted to make love while a crowd of people watched, cheering her on.

- She wanted to take Jim by force, order him to perform oral sex on her, and make him obey her every command.

- She wanted them to take turns tying each other to the bed, to see what it felt like to be at each other's sexual whim.

- She wanted to dress up like a classy call girl, pick Jim up at a hotel bar, then take him home and seduce him.

Although Laura's fantasies were filled with intimate details and symbols unique to her (there were, for example, some very familiar faces among those cheering voyeurs), the themes had much in common with those described by women all over the world. So did her predicament: what to do with the sensual scenarios spilling over her Well of Sexual Dreams. Since Jim took to sexual experimentation like a cow to water, it was up to Laura to discover ways to satisfy her fantasies alone. Sometimes she used a fantasy as a pornographic (and infinitely more compelling) subtext to lovemaking with Jim. Sometimes she used her wild imaginings to turn herself on while she masturbated. Other times she conjured up fantasies when she saw attractive men—and revelled in them until they exhausted themselves.

Fantasies are manifestations of suppressed physical and emotional needs. Laura didn't realize that by exploring her fantasies in a private or masturbatory way she was actually distancing herself from the deep sexual satisfaction she so desired. Nor could she have known that countless women are just like her, fantasizing in the grocery line, filling in the dull spot in their beds with dream lovers created by fertile imaginations. For them—and perhaps for you—the exotic images that unfold between their ears are infinitely more interesting than what happens between the sheets.

What Really Happens in Today's Bedrooms. In one of the most eye-opening and controversial Ann Landers columns ever published, the advice columnist revealed the results of a startling poll. Of the more than one hundred thousand married and/or committed women who voiced their opinion on the subject of sexuality, 72 percent declared they would prefer to end the evening with an affectionate hug rather than a sexual encounter.

Isn't this the land of sexual opportunity? If so, why are so many American women opting to do without "doing it"? One has only to look at the symptoms of sexual dissatisfaction women typically report to see that, for many of the fairer sex, intercourse is only fairly good—and not even close to fulfilling.

Sexual Boredom. An Englishwoman I knew once colorfully tagged this common syndrome "rutting in a rut." And 64 percent of married women in one study report they are doing just that.

Sexual boredom takes two different and equally libido-numbing forms. The same-thing-different-night variety is characterized by a lack of creativity, experimentation, excitement and passion. The sex-on-a-schedule variation (otherwise known as every-Wednesday-night-whether-we-need-it-or-not) is not so much an opportunity for enjoyment as a means for quick, effective physical release. No matter which brand of boredom is plaguing your bed, the result is the same: your sex life will be as flat and bland as a soda cracker.

Sexual Passivity. If you are an erotic mattress potato, if you can't remember the last time you initiated sex with your partner, you are in good company. Many women pinpoint sexual passivity as a symptom of dissatisfaction in their partnerships.

This sort of inertia can stem from a fear of rejection—or from societal conditioning. Whatever its root, you aren't likely to become a truly satisfied woman until you stop waiting for pleasure and start taking the initiative.

Fear of Asking for What You Want in Bed. Imagine that you are in the middle of a sexual encounter but your partner acts like he's in the middle of a race against time. Do you ask him to slow down? Do you suggest that he use a method that is more time consuming, but more pleasurable for you? Or do you simply groan and bear it, hoping that next time will be better? Unless you ask, you aren't likely to receive.

Fear of Letting Go. This isn't just a single symptom of sexual dissatisfaction. It is a blanket term that covers a range of symptoms, including reluctance to be vocally expressive in bed, to vent your feelings, or to use steamy language to enhance the sexual encounter for you and your partner.

Many of the women in my seminars are anything but vocal lovers when they enroll, but they are very talkative about the reasons for their silence. Some fear their partners would be sexually stifled—or confused—by a loud, raucous lover. Others suspect that their silence is a carryover of the childhood edict to speak only when spoken to. Most, however, are haunted by the belief that it is unladylike for a woman to behave as though she is enjoying her intense feelings—even though she is.

Keeping mum about what pleases you is every bit as self-defeating as maintaining silence about what doesn't. Until you are able to pant, groan, or shout out your pleasure, chances are your sex life won't be anything to shout about.

Acting the Part of the Pleaser. If nice girls finish last, it's usually because the guys they're making love with feel free to finish first! Your mother may have told you that sex is primarily for a man's pleasure, not yours. Your friends may have told you that in order to keep a man, you have to do whatever it takes to keep him happy. But I am telling you that unless you make your needs a priority for you, they will never be a priority for your lover.

If sexual boredom is the number one symptom of dissatisfaction, then acting the part of the pleaser gets the dubious honor of second place. But if there were an award for the ultimate pretense to please, that would go to the next symptom.

Faking Orgasm. Recent studies have shown that a surprisingly high percentage of married women—more than two-thirds—fake orgasm periodically during their marriage. For some women, faking the Big O is an infrequent or occasional deception; for others, sadly, it has become part of the routine—as natural an element of lovemaking as their own dissatisfaction.

Research has also shown that women who fake orgasms tend to be those who learned about sex at an earlier age, have had a variety of sexual partners, and know how to achieve climax, both through masturbation and intercourse. In other words, women don't fake because they can't experience pleasure; they do it because they have *chosen* not to experience pleasure.

You may think you are putting on an act to protect your lover's feelings. You may even have convinced yourself (and you can be soooo convincing!) that by manufacturing your own pleasure you will secure your relationship against an affair. Whatever your rationale, you know in your heart that marital stability is not a commodity you can buy at the expense of your own needs. You also know that your deception is cheating you out of your most natural and elemental right: to be truly and blissfully sexually satisfied.

Aside from frustration, the symptoms of sexual dissatisfaction don't add anything to your life, but they *do* add to the Well of Sexual Dreams. It is ironic—and fortuitous—that the urges you repress remain so vividly alive in your mind. Although your fantasies may have developed from years of frustration, they will form the very foundation of your sexual liberation. And although you may feel that your libido has been imprisoned—perhaps for years—your fantasies are the key to unlocking your sexual power. More than any position, more than any sexual technique (even more than an exciting new partner), they are the force that propels you toward everything you ever wanted in bed.

Your Personal Storehouse of Sexual Fantasies. Sexual fantasies are waking dreams in which every thing and every event has an undercurrent of sexual excitement. They are daydreams that turn you on. They are the erotic movies of your mind's eye.

Then again, they are better than the movies! Because these provocative images are projected by the brain—the organ from which *all* sensation stems—your fantasies aren't limited to such basics as sound and color. In fact, they are a feast for all the senses, brimming with exotic smells, tantalizing tastes, touchable textures, stimulating images, changing moods, wondrous settings, intriguing objects, titillating clothing, unique (even bizarre!) sexual acts, dramatic lighting—and, sometimes, a cast of thousands! The prospect of producing just one of these extravaganzas in amazing Sensorama would turn Cecil B. deMille green with envy.

Where do sexual fantasies come from? As you learned from Laura's story, sexual fantasies are pictures painted by your imagination. They are rendered from the rich and limitless palette of your feelings—both the emotions you have collected over the past and the new ones you may experience today or tomorrow. Since your imagination is a limitless medium, you—and every other thinking human being—are capable of creating millions of sexual fantasies during your lifetime. It is no surprise, then, that the Well of Sexual Dreams—the imaginary place in your mind where all of your fantasies are stored—is a boundless source of erotic energy, direction, and stimulation. It is also the secret to becoming a sexually satisfied woman.

Tapping into the Well of Sexual Dreams. Although each of your fantasies may appear to be a totally distinct scenario, all fit together like pieces of a treasure map. Until you assemble that map and reveal it to your partner, he will never be able to touch you the way you need to be touched—to make love to you in a way that fulfills you, emotionally and physically.

To get acquainted with your wellspring of sexual fantasies, and to preview some salient parts of the map that will lead you to erotic ecstasy, I'd like you to try this simple exercise.

Exercise: My Most Exciting Sexual Fantasies

On a sheet of paper, list your most persistently exciting and arousing sexual fantasies: the ones that visit your mind again and again like reliable old friends—even the naughty ones that *feature* old friends!

Since you are already well-acquainted with these scenarios, you can keep your summary brief. Just list a few key descriptive words, or condense the fantasy into a short sentence, then move on to the next scenario.

This is an opportunity to get in touch with the erotic images already swimming around in your Well of Sexual Dreams, so don't try to create new fantasies right now. List only those fantasies you have entertained (and that have entertained you!) before. Take about fifteen minutes if you need it, but don't spend much more time than that.

Refreshing, wasn't it? Dipping into the Well always is!

If you are like most of the women who have attended my seminars, you've written down at least a handful of fantasies—perhaps four or five—or maybe as many as ten or twenty. Good! The closer you are to your fantasies, the closer you are to sexual fulfillment. Now check back over your list and pick out any recurring themes or sexual scenarios that seem especially arousing. If, for instance, your erotic dreams are filled with exciting images of playful bondage, sexual bossiness, or pleasurable aggression, then power—or your lack of it—is an issue you will want to explore later in this program. If, on the other hand, sex with an improper stranger is a scenario that comes to call as regularly as the mailman, you might give some thought to what your dream man has to offer that your partner does not. (Hint: it's usually mind-blowing, limit-breaking erotic freedom.)

Finally, go through the list once again and ask yourself how many are fantasies that you have admitted to your partner. If the tally is significantly less than the total number on your list, you are concealing your sexual dreams not only from yourself but from the person who can help you use them to their best advantage.

Of course, you may have listed only one erotic dream, or even none. If you did, you are not alone. Many women, Laura included, have become world-class repressors. They suppress not only their urges but the fantasies that spring from those urges. But that doesn't mean the Well of Sexual Dreams has run dry. Whether you are aware of it or not, whether you think of yourself as sexually creative or not, there are thousands of erotic, arousing images swimming around right now deep in your mind. This simple, enjoyable program will put you in touch with this precious part of yourself—and put the secret to deep, invigorating release directly within your reach.

Becoming—and Staying—Sexually Satisfied in a Sexually Repressive Society. Your eyes may be the windows to your soul, but your fantasies are the doorway to total sexual satisfaction. Wild or whimsical, romantic or randy, they remind you—literally dozens of times each day—of the exquisite pleasure you are capable of. And that's not all. Just as the emotions you feel and the thoughts you think form the nature of your personality, the sensual scenarios that whirl in your mind form the essence of your undiscovered sexuality. Because your fantasies are your uncensored creations, they reflect without distortion your image of the unbridled pleasure potential within you right now. And because your erotic dreams are visualizations of your real desires and needs, they foreshadow your emergence into a lifetime of passion and satisfaction.

The ability to tap into and share sexual fantasies—for your pleasure and your lover's—is the basis for getting everything you want in bed. It is also the foundation of this program. When Mother Nature endowed you with an endlessly productive and creative imagination, she graciously provided you with all the mechanisms you need to achieve lasting satisfaction. This book is a tool enabling you to take advantage of those mechanisms, bring a dynamic new dimension to your lovemaking, and make you the lusty, adventurous sexual dynamo in the bedroom that you are in your wildest dreams.

3 ~

The Sexual Satisfaction Training Program: Five Steps to Erotic Ecstasy

~

If you are like most of the women who attend my seminars, it has taken years of ongoing sexual frustration to bring you to this point—and to this book. My Five-Step Program was developed with two objectives in mind. The first is to put the power to enrich, enlighten, and liberate your sex life directly into your hands, to put you in full control of the pleasure you receive. The second is to set your sexual fantasies free—to bring them out of your mind and into the bedroom, where they can transform your intimate relationship, emancipate your libido, and turn your bedroom into a magical stage where all of your secret erotic dreams come true. Some of these results are immediately attainable. Their transformational power will begin to work the very night you introduce the corresponding technique. Others can undo a lifetime of dissatisfaction in only weeks—or even days.

These can seem like lofty goals, I know—especially if you are looking at them from the sexual equivalent of rock bottom. To you, I say, you have to aim high to hit the highs! Receiving sexual pleasure elevates your mood and boosts your confidence. Since this program is literally a pleasure every step of the way, all you have to do is begin and you're halfway there.

But where do you begin to change the inhibitions of a lifetime? This program begins with the LoveSkills Makeover—a proven-effective method for educating your partner to your sexual hot spots. A powerful hands-on technique that puts your man in touch with your erogenous zones, the LoveSkills Makeover teaches him what it takes to bring you to the dizzying heights of pleasure every time you make love.

The second step is the PowerTease Method—the ultimate antidote for sexual boredom. Used as directed, PowerTeasing brings out the savage in your man, rewards him in very tangible ways for his sexual compliance, and gets him so turned on that he will do absolutely anything to make *you* happy in bed.

Wild Night may mark the middle of the program, but as an erotic experience, it is anything but middle-of-the-road! A sizzling scenario that puts you in full control of the bedroom, a red-hot happening that fulfills his fantasies and yours, Wild Night is the night you light a fire under your love life—and use your inhibitions and his macho resistance as kindling!

Seeing a woman change from a passive, pliant lover to a randy, sexual dynamo is a treat for any man, but *hearing* all about the fabulous fantasies that energize her libido is the ultimate turn-on! In step four of the program, fantasy-sharing, you will stimulate your partner's most sensitive erogenous zone—his imagination—by expressing during lovemaking all the fabulous fantasies that drive you wild. Your fantasies aren't just random

daydreams; they are the emotional fixtures that pinpoint and illuminate the most direct route to sexual
satisfaction. Step four of this unique program reveals
how, by bringing your fantasies out of your head and
into your bedroom, you can reestablish intimacy with
the man you love and build a spontaneous, erotically
evolved sex life that will keep you satisfied forever.

But even that's only the beginning. Step five, play-
acting, opens the door onto an entirely new dimension
of lovemaking, where your most intriguing, arousing
fantasies become *real*. With the help of this book, you
will physically enact, with your lover, the powerful scenarios that give voice to your deepest, most intimate
feelings. And in the safety and comfort of your own
bedroom, you will bring dramatically to life all of the
passionate women you are: the temptress, the innocent,
the erotic adventurer, the tease, the vixen . . . and, of
course, the sexually satisfied woman within you.

What's in a Word? Power. Control. Emancipation. It
may seem strange to you to encounter strong, politically charged words like these in a guide to sexual fulfillment. It may even seem a bit ironic in a book that
goes head to head with a male-dominated, sexually repressive society that continues to wield power and control over women. Am I suggesting that you turn the
tables and become a sexual oppressor yourself? Not at
all. I assure you your partner will receive more than his
share of pleasure by virtue of your sexual liberation.

But make no mistake about it: this book was written
primarily for *your* pleasure and *your* ultimate satisfaction. It is, without apology, a book about control—not
an oppressive control you brandish over an unwilling
partner, but control over your own sexual destiny. It is

also a book about knowledge, education, action, openness, liberation, power and compassion. These powerful tenets, which I call the Seven Principles of Sexual Satisfaction, are the true cornerstones of erotic self-realization.

THE SEVEN PRINCIPLES

Knowledge. Sexually speaking, all you need to know is this: Know yourself, and you will know what pleases you; allow your partner to know you, and he will know *how* to please you!

Although it may take a lifetime to acquire it, self-knowledge is an enduring gift that enhances your life in innumerable ways. Of course, this book deals with knowledge in the biblical sense: that is to say, sexual intimacy. Since mine is a feel-good program, and because feeling good means accepting your desires and fantasies without conditions or judgment, this program won't just make you more knowledgeable about what pleases you; it will make you happier, in bed and out.

Education. "Does he really think it feels good when he does that?" "How would he like it if I yanked his penis like he does my breasts?" "Two minutes of foreplay—one minute of intercourse. That's my sex life, in a nutshell."

My clients, some of whom I have quoted above, have transformed my private practice into an in-depth, twenty-year continuing-education course on what does—and does not—excite a woman. In the spirit of spreading the excitement, my Five-Step Program shares with you the private practices and intimate techniques that will educate your partner to the inner workings of your body and mind.

Your lover may think of himself as a sex machine, but unless you let him know what makes your engine hum, he is a machine operating at half capacity! Teaching your partner all about yourself and your sexual needs lubricates the inner workings of your relationship, tunes up passionate partnerships that have gotten out of sync, and gets your erotic pistons firing in unison.

Your partner is the "other half" of your quest for pleasure. Unless you put him in the know about your innermost desires, you simply cannot position yourself for enduring sexual satisfaction.

Action. Sexual desire minus passionate action equals . . . frustration!

It's no coincidence that the word *action* is a prominent part of *satisfaction*—and one of the keystones of this program. Sex is an active endeavor. Lie back passively during an erotic encounter and you cannot really control what happens in the bedroom. You may reach orgasm, but you will never achieve the deep emotional and physical release of total sexual fulfillment.

Action defines itself: it literally means to act on. By working through my Five-Step Program, you will find that you will act on your sexual feelings more often, initiate sex more frequently, clearly assert your needs and desires, and actively take the pleasure you need to become a satisfied woman in bed. In short, you will become an energetic, erotic go-getter. And that's a heck of a lot better than settling for whatever bits and pieces of pleasure a lover decides to give you.

Openness. If you could have one wish for your sex life right now, what would it be? If you can express that wish to your partner—or if you can visualize yourself doing so as a result of this program—openness is within your reach.

In terms of your sexuality, openness can best be defined as intercourse without inhibition. Of course, intercourse comes in two wonderful varieties: verbal and physical. When both kinds are present in a relationship, the two work in tandem to establish a sense of intimacy—or mutual openness—between committed partners. Because this book enables you to open yourself completely to your lover, to reveal all your secret sexual desires and thoughts, it also opens the door to a new kind of intimacy: intimacy without guilt, without inhibition, and without end.

Liberation. Plant the seed of self-revelation, nurture it with liberal doses of pleasure, and what begins as openness quickly blossoms into full-blown liberation. Whether you define sexual freedom as emancipation from the repressive dictates of society or release from your own inhibitions, your liberation will be a natural and gratifying offshoot of the Five-Step Program.

Behind every sexual fantasy is a pent-up feeling. This program sets those feelings free! When a person is emancipated from her hidden emotions, what she commonly experiences (outside of sheer physical ecstasy) is a wave of relief, followed by an enduring sense of control, strength, and inner growth. The formal term for this kind of personal change is "self-actualization." I would modify that here to read "sexual self-actualization." This program enables you to actualize—or fulfill—your sexual nature, leaving you free to move forward into areas of greater growth—and more powerful forms of sexual expression. Which leads us directly to one of the most central and controversial principles of this program.

Power. When have women known power in the bedroom? The most cursory glance through the history books will show you that the traditionally acceptable woman's role—in bed and out—has been that of the passive pleaser. Even Eve, the first woman audacious enough to independently select and devour the apple of her eye, was duly punished for her power play. Not only was she required to wear a scratchy fig leaf (the height of anaphrodisiac chic), she was ostracized and evicted to boot.

Of course, in manipulative or exploitative hands, power is the ultimate weapon. Whether men hoard power because they enjoy wielding it themselves or because they want to keep it from others is a point that has been argued vigorously for years. But in terms of your life and your burgeoning sexuality, there is only one truth—and it is inarguable: without power, without direct access to the energizing life force that *is* sexuality, it is impossible to attain sexual fulfillment.

Just as the three equal sides of a triangle come together to give this form its distinctive shape, three kinds of power shape your sexual destiny: the power to be, the power to create, and the power to control. The first—the power to be—is the foundation upon which the others rest.

Otherwise known as the great "I Am," the power to be is the self-determinate energy that inspires you to assert the person you are, to do what you want in bed, to make things happen in a way that will affirm your individuality and bring you pleasure. Clearly, developing this kind of power can create some difficulties. The will to be depends on your willingness to take risks, to courageously pit your desires against your fears, to test the strength of your convictions against your partner's. Oftentimes the need for individuality and the desire for love can make for strange bedfellows. Still, this elemental force is the mainstay of a strong sense of self—and that is always positive.

Put the power to be into motion and you have the second side of the triangle, the power to create. It is rooted in your desire for erotic self-determination—the urge to express your libido in a creative way, to actively set up and fulfill the limitless sexual destiny you crave. It is not without effort, but with a guide like this one, you can turn that effort into play.

Because the third type of power—control—requires a certain amount of power over your partner, it is the most commonly misunderstood and misused element of the power triangle. Obviously, no one enjoys being taken advantage of or used. If you manipulate your partner like a sex toy, or use him to fulfill your desires without regard to his needs, you are more likely to achieve an argument than win intimacy.

Compassion. Tempering your power with compassion lets you bring out the best in your lover, share the euphoria of liberation with him, and make sex as exciting and satisfying as it can be for both of you.

Power in its most positive form always goes hand in hand with responsibility. By seasoning your passion with compassion, by using your power to stimulate not dominate, you make your lover a willing accomplice in your quest for sexual satisfaction—and that's the kind of partner in crime you can blissfully do time with!

In the pages to come you will see how these seven principles work together to bring about a single goal: satisfaction. Total satisfaction. *Your* satisfaction. If you are like most other women who have used this program to reenergize their intimate lives, you will also see how your sexual fulfillment spawns renewed romanticism, erotic exuberance, and a lasting feeling of confidence and well-being.

So hang onto your hat (it will come in handy when you begin acting out your fantasies!). The time has come to turn the page on frustration. It's time to become a sexually satisfied woman.

4 ~

The LoveSkills Makeover: Teaching Your Man What Turns You On

~

- Sex with my partner has become boring and routine for me. What can I do to spice it up?

- My husband finishes just when I'm getting started. How can I get him to slow down so I can enjoy sex, too?

- Emotionally, my partner is my closest companion. But sexually I feel he doesn't know me at all! How can I talk to him about my sexual needs?

- I've been faking orgasms for fifteen years. Of course, my husband doesn't know. But I'd certainly prefer to experience the real thing. . . .

- How can I get the man I love to touch me where I want to be touched and the way I want to be touched without hurting his feelings?

Like a lot of people, I smile to myself every time I hear the Beatles song, "All You Need Is Love." Unlike a lot of people, who may not deal with the symptoms of dissatisfaction every day, I smile because I've learned that love *isn't* all you need—not if what you've got in mind is mind-blowing, knee-weakening sex!

Of course, sex is a lot more than a physical act. If it weren't, sex without intimacy wouldn't leave us feeling empty; indiscriminate sex wouldn't leave us feeling used; and orgasm without satisfaction wouldn't exist. Even the swingingest singles I know will admit that intercourse is most gratifying when it is a physical celebration between two people who share a powerful emotional connection.

Earlier in this book I mentioned that sex is an act that begins between the ears and ends between the sheets. If you took the time to immerse yourself in your Well of Sexual Dreams, you have experienced for yourself how fantasies work to increase your desire for and enjoyment of sex. It's also true that too many people—women and men alike—place too much emphasis on orgasm without paying enough attention to emotional foreplay. Sex is, after all, an act that requires us to get naked with each other, literally and figuratively. Unless you're giving your lover liberal doses of trust, intimacy, respect, and communication during the day, you simply can't expect him to be bubbling over with sexual energy come sundown.

It's safe to say that every woman who has picked up this book knows that sex can be a profoundly powerful part of a happy ongoing relationship. Many have learned by experience that it can be equally powerful when it is *not* physically fulfilling. The absence of physical pleasure—even a temporary dry spell—tends to put distance between otherwise loving mates. Within weeks or sometimes days, they grow accustomed to feeling at arm's length from each other, and the resumption of intimacy seems a daunting task. The outright denial of physical pleasure—by one partner or another—is a power play that leads to conflict, extramarital affairs, and even divorce.

Biology Is Destiny. The body of evidence is clear: the biological urge for lusty, lascivious pleasure is what inspires us to turn to each other for emotional and physical release. And since knowledge of your biology has everything to do with your sexual destiny, it is crucial that you learn as much about your body as you can—then share what you've learned with your partner so he can touch you, arouse you, and lift you to peak after sexual peak.

This chapter, which introduces my unique LoveSkills Makeover, will enable you to educate your partner to the ways and means of your body. Through this simple and pleasurable method, you will teach him to make love to you in the most tantalizing ways imaginable—to draw from your body's secret places the most exquisite sensations your sexuality can bestow. In short, you will turn the man you love into the lover of your dreams.

You may feel that your partner is a good lover already. Or you may feel that your man has his heart in the right place, but his hands, fingers and lips tend to miss the mark. It really doesn't matter how much your partner can thrill you in bed. The LoveSkills Makeover rewards him erotically for doing what *you* know makes you feel best; you will only enhance your pleasure during sex, and the love act will be that much more exciting for you.

Before I show you how to use the LoveSkills Makeover to educate your partner to the ways of your body, I'd like you to become familiar with your own body. If you discover your most sensitive areas and what makes you feel best, you can pass that knowledge on to your partner. You may already know your body very well, know what pleases you sexually and sensually (through all the senses), but I'd still like you to become intimately familiar with your most pleasurable sensations, and where you feel them, so you will know where to direct your partner when we get to the training technique.

Accordingly, here are two Preliminary Exercises to get you in touch with the pleasures of your body as intimately as is possible on your own.

Preliminary Exercise 1: *Love Comes to Every Body*

This exercise combines fantasy and visualization to give you a mind's-eye view of each part of the body that gives you sensual pleasure, and the ways you'd prefer those areas to be stroked in order to produce the maximum effect. Emotion is an important part of this scenario: rather than thinking of your body as a collection of individual parts, try to view each area as you do during lovemaking—as part of a whole, energized with passion and emotion. This exercise is best performed at home in bed, when you're alone and relaxed.

Lie down in bed on your back (for best results, unclothed), with the lights off.

Now close your eyes, breathe deeply and count to ten slowly. By the end of the count you should be more relaxed than you were at the start. If you still feel wound up, breathe deeply and count to ten once more. Do this as many times as you like until every muscle in your body feels limp, heavy, and very, very relaxed.

Starting with your head, imagine your partner making love to every inch of your body. Visualize him caressing your hair, using any of the natural gifts of his body: his hands, his mouth, his penis, or any other part that stimulates you. Concentrate on how it feels to have your hair stroked, kissed, gently pulled, warmed by your lover's breath, or traversed with his mouth. You can even imagine him brushing it, or smoothing it with lingering fingerstrokes.

Now imagine your partner making love to your head, massaging your scalp, kissing it, licking it, or rubbing it with whatever parts of his body feel best in your mind.

Savoring each delicious sensation, allow your lover to work his way down to your forehead, eyebrows, eyes, nose, cheeks, ears, mouth, chin, and neck. The neck usually is a very sensuous area. Imagine him massaging it, teasing it with his tongue, kissing it, running his fingernails along it, even rubbing his penis over it.

Continue in this way, proceeding slowly down your body, imagining your partner making love to one area at a time: your shoulders, breasts, nipples, arms, forearms and wrists, hands, fingers, stomach, hips, bottom, vagina, clitoris, thighs, knees, calves and lower legs, ankles, feet, and, finally, your toes.

When you have drawn every bit of pleasure you can from this exercise, make a mental note of the areas that were most sensitive and the ways you most enjoyed having them stimulated in your mind. Better yet, write your observations down or record them into a tape recorder during the exercise. (Extreme pleasure isn't known to be a memory enhancer!)

Whatever happens, *do not touch yourself during this exercise*. Although your physical responses may be very real, this exercise is strictly an imaginary one. And be

sure to spend lots of time on each area of your body.
Don't be in a rush to get the exercise over with. Find
out what you really like, at least mentally. You will
probably find that it will be very similar to what you
enjoy physically.

When you have finished with the exercise and re-
corded your findings, go back up your body if you wish,
or imagine your partner gently turning you over and
making love to the back side of your body: the nape of
your neck, your spine, the area beneath your shoulder
blades, your anal area (if you wish), the backs of your
knees, and the bottoms of your feet. This process
should leave you feeling very relaxed yet invigorated, if
not downright stimulated. It should also leave you with
a sense of confidence and well-being about your body
and its unlimited potential as a source of pleasure. Now
proceed with the next exercise, which will put you literally in touch with your physical attributes.

Preliminary Exercise 2: Hands-on Learning

In this exercise you're going to become acquainted
with your body in a much more intimate way than in
Preliminary Exercise 1. While in that exercise you only
imagined having different areas of your body made love
to, here you are going to touch the different areas of
your body, to get a firsthand account of the sensations
you enjoy most.

Of course, this is not the same as having your partner do the stimulation. Because you cannot duplicate
the eroticism of having another person touch you—
especially the man you love—the sensations won't be
nearly as acute. (Nor will you enjoy that delicious element of surprise that comes with lovemaking *à deux*.)

Still, this exercise will give you hands-on knowledge of where your skin is most sensitive, where your sensual feelings are most intense, and the ways you like to be touched—information that can reap big dividends once it's passed on to your lover.

I do encourage you to use your hands during this exercise (there's nothing like skin-to-skin contact, especially when you're doing some sensual information gathering) but if you own a vibrator, you may use that as well. This is a book about sexual liberation, so feel free to perform the exercise in the way that benefits you most.

As for masturbation, which is a common and enjoyable side effect of this technique, well . . . just go with the flow. But keep in mind that your main goal is to discover what parts of your body respond most intensely to touch. You will more than likely find that the same areas you find most erotic when touching yourself are those that you most enjoy having stimulated when you're making love with your partner.

Once again, this is an exercise to be performed at home, preferably in bed. Since it requires concentration and the ability to touch yourself for a period of time, undisturbed, you will probably want to do it when your partner is not at home.

Lie down on the bed, with your clothes off and the lights out. Close your eyes and breathe deeply while slowly counting to ten. As you did in the previous exercise, repeat this procedure as many times as you need in order to feel fully relaxed. If you wish to use a vibrator during the exercise, have it handy.

When you are completely relaxed, begin stroking your hair—gently, or firmly, or however is most pleasurable for you. Concentrate on the sensual feelings your fingers transmit to your head as well as those that flow from your hair to your fingers.

Keeping your eyes closed, concentrating fully on the area under your touch, begin caressing, stroking, and massaging your scalp. Does it feel better when you use your nails or just the pads of your fingers? Which parts of it respond most intensely to loving attention? All areas of the scalp are not created equal, as far as sensitivity is concerned. This is what you need to discover about every nook, cranny, and inner and outer part of your body.

Continue with the back of your neck. This probably is a very responsive, even erotic, area for you. Now move on to your forehead, eyebrows, eyes, nose, cheeks, ears (do you enjoy stroking behind your ears?), mouth, chin, and neck.

Spend lots of time on each area—don't rush it. Remember, you're trying to learn what gives you the most pleasure. When you find an area you particularly like, focus on it for a while. Stay with the feeling; concentrate on what about it you like. Try different modes of touch: vary the pressure and the stroke, or alternate between using the soft pads of your fingers and your nails. Remember, the sexiness that your partner feels when you use your nails can stimulate you, too.

Continue with your shoulders and then your breasts. Spend a lot of time on your breasts, finding exactly how you like to be touched and stroked there. Find the exact touch and pressure you like on your nipples.

Move on to your stomach, your sides, your back. Then work your way down your arms, one at a time, starting with your upper arm, then the inside of your elbow, your forearm, wrist, hand, and ending with your fingers and thumb.

Now caress your hips, thighs, buttocks, and your vaginal area. Of course, it will be difficult to find out exactly how you like to be touched on, in, and around your vagina and clitoris without being tremendously stimulated. And you probably already know how you like being touched there, especially if you allow yourself to masturbate periodically. But explore further this time: try finding areas you don't often stimulate, or have never stimulated. Try to stop short of masturbating so you can allow the pleasurable feelings to build, as they do during lovemaking. But if the mood strikes you, stimulate yourself to orgasm, then continue to seek out new ways to pleasure your genitals. It's your body: explore!

When you are finished, move on to your anal area, if you like. You may find that this offers very pleasant sensations—even feel motivated to insert a finger into yourself. Be careful though. Never insert a finger into your vagina after putting it into your anus without washing first with soap and warm water, as you can introduce bacteria into your vagina that can cause infection.

Finally, stroke and stimulate your legs, beginning with your thighs. Focus on your inner thighs (this should be a very sensitive area), then move on to your knees, especially the backs of your knees, your calves and lower legs, your ankles, feet, toes, and, finally, the bottoms of your feet.

You can repeat the exercise, going up your body, or end it now by breathing deeply while counting to ten, then opening your eyes. By now you should be fully relaxed, fully at ease, somewhat tingly, and possibly very stimulated. You will certainly be invigorated by this physical and mental self-massage.

Again, make a mental note of what you found most stimulating. You may also write it down, or consider using a tape recorder while the exercise is under way.

Your lover will never become totally at ease with your body until you are. (Self-consciousness in a lover turns into hesitancy, sexual shyness, or passivity during lovemaking—and none of these attributes is likely to make your satisfaction quotient rise.) I suggest you repeat the Preliminary Exercises until you feel perfectly at ease with your body and perfectly knowledgeable in the ways of its sensual pleasures. Remember, whatever you gain here is information you are going to subtly pass on to your partner, to enable him to become the lover you want him to be. Imagine him stimulating those parts of your body you found most sensitive to pleasure—and in exactly the ways you want them to be stimulated! This will happen as you move along in the LoveSkills Makeover.

THE LOVESKILLS TECHNIQUE

Before you send a message, it is crucial that you know what you intend to say. Having performed the two Preliminary Exercises, you now have an idea of the sexual secrets you want to telegraph to your lover. It's time to send that carnal communiqué—and there's no more enjoyable way than through the three steps of the LoveSkills technique:

1. Get him to do what you want
2. Tell him how good it feels, then . . .
3. Get him to do it even better!

The pivot on which the LoveSkills technique turns is that of *communication*. Specifically, you will be giving your partner *communication that rewards*.

We all like a little positive reinforcement in return for a job well done—and that goes double for our performances in the sexual arena. Whether it's a verbal pat on the back or a physical pat on the backside, reward is inspiring! With the LoveSkills method you reward your partner *before* he does what you want him to do, so he has an incentive to comply with your wishes. Then, because you reward him *after* he successfully does what you want, he has inducement to keep on pleasing you. And since you will *continue* to reward him throughout the sexual experience, he will practice his technique until perfect—until he can play your body like a beautifully tuned violin.

Before going further, I want to point out that this method takes time. It is imperative that you introduce the LoveSkills technique on a night (or afternoon) when erotic matters can take priority. The LoveSkills Makeover is not a quickie technique. It isn't meant for a night when you're making love twenty minutes before you plan to go to sleep. A tight schedule not only will hinder your ability to experiment with verbal rewards, it will prevent you from savoring the undivided attention of your lover. The resulting encounter would be as satisfying as bolting down a meal prepared by a four-star chef.

If your partner always initiates sex, or the two of you always make love at the same time, try to devote at least an hour to the lovemaking so you will have the time and patience for trial and error. Remember: it has taken years for your lover to form his sexual habits. It's worth an hour of your time to change them. Now on to the specifics of this method.

Step 1: Get Him to Do What You Want

It is a well-known maxim in business that would-be executives should put themselves in the vicinity of success. Now that you're getting down to business with the man you love, it's imperative that you put him in the general area where he can perform successfully, too!

Whether you kept the data in your mind or in a journal, the two Preliminary Exercises provided you with a comprehensive guide to your most sensitive erogenous zones, as well as a step-by-step description of the strokes, touches and modes of stimulation most likely to bring you satisfaction. All you need to do now is put your lover on the map by directing him to the parts of your body and the specific techniques that will bring you the most pleasure.

To put him in the know, begin with a statement something like this:

It feels so good when you _____ (kiss my breasts, squeeze my nipples, kiss me down there, touch me in back, rub my thighs, etc.)

Bear in mind that your goal at this point is to put your man in the right area—within reach, so to speak, of the techniques that will enhance your satisfaction.

For example, suppose you very much enjoy having him squeeze your nipples. You say, "Oh, it feels so good when you squeeze my nipples." He responds by zeroing in on the tip of your breast. You've got him in the general vicinity of where you want him. It should not concern you if his touch seems a little rough, or his aim is a little skewed. There is plenty of time for fine-tuning later.

Notice what you are saying when you use the phrase, "It feels so good when you squeeze my nipples." Before he even begins the activity, you are verbally rewarding him for his efforts by complimenting him on an activity that you know pleases you. Remember: you are trying to get him to do something you really *want* him to do, something you *know* you will enjoy based on what you learned in the two Preliminary Exercises. There is nothing more exciting to a man than to see his partner genuinely respond to his touch. When you say, "It feels so good when you squeeze my nipples," you are promising him that he will be able to witness your pleasure. The thought of seeing you respond to something he does will tantalize him—and *make* him want to engage in the suggested activity.

Positive reinforcement is not a passive way to manipulate a lover into doing it your way. It is an active yet nonthreatening technique for asserting your sexual needs. Of course, as you progress through the program your requests will become more aggressive—even salty. But initial statements like, "I love it when you . . ." or "It really turns me on when you . . ." are designed to get you into the swing of sexual expression—and to introduce your partner to the rewards of taking pleasure from your pleasure.

Hit . . . or Miss. If, after your direction, he is not near where you want him to be, or if he is not performing the act you have encouraged him to, then it will take a little more effort on your part to move him the way you want him to "move" you.

If, for example, he is stroking your breasts and your genitals are screaming for attention, you can repeat the initial reward statement: "It feels so good when you touch me down there." For most men, "it feels so good" will be the magic phrase that opens his mind to your request. But if verbal direction is not enough to get him to do what you want, you may want to get physical and actively "position" him to maximize your pleasure.

Positioning is both a verbal *and a physical* technique. And because it leaves no doubt that your immediate needs are not being met, you must use it very carefully so you don't offend or threaten your partner. A typical positioning gesture would be to gently—and sensitively—put your hand on his, then begin to move it toward the area you wish stimulated.

There is a rule, however, about using physical gestures to get your partner to do what you want: unless you know that your partner likes to have you direct him in this way, NEVER USE A PHYSICAL GESTURE WITHOUT SIMULTANEOUSLY OFFERING A VERBAL REWARD. This is particularly true in this initial LoveSkills training stage, when a partner who is unaccustomed to sexual direction may be confounded by—or put off by—the new assertive you.

If, for instance, he is stroking your thighs and you want him to perform oral sex on you, first reward him verbally for what he is doing: "The way you're touching me feels so good, I want even more of you." Then, gently caressing his head with your hands, you can urge him in the direction of your genitals, saying: "I've been waiting all day for you to kiss and lick me down there. Don't make me wait any longer!"

Of course, no one likes to be forced to do something they really don't want to do—or to be manipulated into an act they might enjoy but are not ready for at the moment. The goal here is to tantalize—not terrorize. In the initial stages of the LoveSkills Makeover, it is important to experiment with ways to signal your intentions—both verbally and physically—without seeming pushy, demanding, or bossy. In time, the subtle approach will give way to more uninhibited love-making—with your lover's enthusiastic participation! But for the time being, it's best if you aren't any more aggressive with your partner than you would want him to be with you.

If at First You Don't Succeed . . . If your verbal statements seem to be falling on deaf ears and all your efforts to move your partner seem to be meeting with an irresistible counterforce, you can try to position your body so that the areas you want stimulated are within his reach.

Of course, your movements should be very sensual and fluid at this stage. Don't, for example, throw your hands up in frustration, flop yourself into position and cry, "Here! For goodness sakes, touch me here!" But don't be afraid to move yourself around to get your "naughty bits" near his hand, lips, or penis. If you feel particularly confident, and cunnilingus is on your mind, you can even playfully straddle his chest while he's lying on his back and slowly inch up towards his mouth. As you do so, offer verbal rewards: "This feels so good. I'm really getting turned on." You can even tease him: "Should I go farther?"

Risky Business . . . can be fun! This is your golden opportunity to take everything you learned from the Preliminary Exercises and apply it in the bedroom, so don't be afraid to take chances and encourage your partner to explore all the interesting nooks and hidden crannies of your body. Remote places—and taboo places—can be pleasurable spots for sexual adventurers to visit, especially if they've never been there before! You may discover a destination worth writing home about. And you're sure to find that your explorations are much more stimulating with a companion along.

"If it feels good, do it!" might have been the battle cry of the sexual revolution, but if you want to bring about a revolution in your bedroom, try . . .

Step 2: If It Feels Good, Tell Him So

"If my wife [girlfriend] would only tell me what she wants when I'm making love to her!" "She makes sounds . . . but is she satisfied? Who can tell?" "What *do* women want in bed? I wish I knew."

A mysterious seductress who tantalizes every man she meets with exotic secrets is the stuff fantasies are made of. But not knowing what pleases a woman, or whether he is pleasing her at all, drives a man crazy!

Judging from my male clients, some of whom I've quoted above, a man wants nothing more than to know what his partner wants, where and how she wants to be stimulated, and exactly what is going to drive her wild with pleasure. Why? Because making a woman feel good makes a man feel good about himself as a lover!

Step 2 of the LoveSkills Makeover is a classic win–win situation. Your man will get what he wants most: the reassurance he needs to be the best lover he can be. And you will get all the stimulation you want, just the way you want it.

Assume that your partner took the cue from your first verbal reward ("It feels so good when you . . .") and is now performing the act you wanted him to. Assuming that his efforts are pleasurable for you, the time is right to boost his confidence and bolster his motivation by giving him a second verbal reward. For instance:

- Oh, that feels so good!

- You do that so well!

- That's just the way I like it.

- Oh, yes, that's it—that's just the right spot.

- You really know how to make me feel good.

- You're such a great lover!

Of course, you should only use a rewarding statement if you *are* experiencing pleasure. *Do not* fake it. *Ever.* Verbally rewarding him for something that is not enjoyable for you simply reinforces his misguided ideas of what turns you on sexually, and that will only prolong your feelings of sexual dissatisfaction. If the activity isn't taking you where you want to go, repeat the verbal or physical repositioning techniques. Then, when the feeling is just right . . .

Lie Back and Enjoy It! Allow yourself to savor the warmth of your lover's touch. Revel in the way your back arches in response to his caress. Eager for more? Of course you are. But don't be in a hurry to move the lovemaking forward. This is your chance to focus on the pleasure your partner is giving you, to float along languidly on wave after wave of building intensity, to enjoy the rousing feeling of his breath on your neck, his erect penis against your leg.

It is also your opportunity to keep the momentum going by providing your man with an erotic play-by-play that will stimulate his most powerful erogenous zone of all: his mind.

Turn Up the Volume. Moans, groans, and squeals of pleasure don't cut it in conversation, but the primordial sounds that constitute pillow talk send a wildly gratifying message in the bedroom. Of course, I'm not suggesting that you exaggerate your pleasure—that only reinforces what may be lackluster or lazy technique. But genuine "oohs" and "aahs"—as well as some steamy words of encouragement—are the ultimate positive feedback. At the very least, they will motivate your man to continue the stimulation. At their most effective, your sexy sounds will set off a wildly passionate sensual spiral. He pleasures you, so you reward him. He stimulates you more ardently; you let him know you appreciate the effort. He turns up the heat; you add fuel to the fire. And . . . well, you get the picture.

The key in this stage is to be expressive—and that means letting your partner know exactly how you're feeling, especially at the pivotal points of the encounter. If he is stimulating you in a new and exciting way, send him the message that you admire his ingenuity. If what he is doing is bringing you close to orgasm, announce the good news! Shout, pant, or scream, "I'm going to come [have an orgasm] soon!" The seconds before your orgasm is a very important point for a man. It lets him know that he has brought you to the brink of climax, and that he will be treated to the ultimate erotic show: watching you writhe in uncontrollable ecstasy beneath his touch.

Getting everything you want in bed means getting it *your* way. In the third part of the LoveSkills Makeover you'll fine-tune your partner's lovemaking until it is exactly—in the words of the Bard—as you like it.

Step 3: Get Him to Do It Even Better!

Ah, LoveSkills ... what a motivator! It can coax even the most resistant men to go with the flow. If that's the effect this method has had on your partner, you've probably already used the verbal reward system to do some preliminary fine-tuning of your lover's technique. If so, good for you! A kind word—and an enticing erotic suggestion—is often all it takes to get him to "kiss you here" and "run his tongue over there."

But satisfying sex is a dynamic experience. In the throes of passion, you may decide that a different type of stimulation (different from the one you're getting) would fly you to the moon. It may occur to you that you'd like to explore a new experience altogether. Or you may simply need to bring your partner closer to the activity you suggested in the first place. That's when you need to pull Step 3 out of your bag of tricks: to get him to do what he's doing *exactly* the way you want him to do it.

Suppose your partner has been manually stroking your vagina, as you directed him to, but what you want now is for him to brush his fingers lightly along your clitoris. In Step 1, you would have said something like, "Oh, if you would only use those sensitive fingers on my vagina, it would feel so good." Maybe you guided his hand to the pleasurable spot. Then, in Step 2, you would have rewarded him verbally by expressing the pleasure it gave you when he touched you the way you wanted him to: "Oh, that's it—that really turns me on!" Now, in Step 3, you fine-tune his abilities by redirecting him—verbally or physically, or both ("It feels really good when you stroke me lightly right there!"), then following up with a verbal reward ("Yes, that's it! Oh, that feels so good. You do that so well.").

Much to many men's chagrin, women don't come with easily reachable "joy buttons" that put them into immediate sexual bliss. Fine-tuning can take some time—and several adjustments. Suppose, for example, that prior to Step 1 your lover was kissing you when you would have preferred him to be performing oral sex on you. For Step 1, you would have said something like, "It feels really good when you kiss me down there." In Step 2, you would have rewarded him verbally for pleasuring you in the general way you requested: "Oh, that feels *so* nice!"

Now suppose that the sexual activity you requested isn't as satisfying as you know it could be—and you have some very definite ideas on how to make it better. To fine-tune his pleasuring technique, you simply need to return to Step 1 and get him to do what you want, this time offering specific direction about the type of stimulation that would feel best to you. ("It really feels good when you move your tongue up and down my clitoris.") As always, follow up a job well done with a verbal reward (Step 2).

Sex is not a one-shot deal. You can continue the direction/reward dialogue as long as you wish (or as long as your lover holds out!). If, for instance, you wanted to further fine-tune the above scenario, you might say something like, "It feels so good when you nibble me right there" (Step 1), then verbally reward him (Step 2) when he does it right ("Oh, that tickles—but it feels so good!").

With patience and imagination, you could go on indefinitely, using the three-step LoveSkills Makeover to focus your lover's attention on your obvious hot spots: your breasts, nipples, vagina, clitoris, and anal area. Or you could concentrate his efforts on the more subtle erogenous zones you discovered during the Preliminary Exercises: your neck, shoulders, inner thighs, bottom, hips, back, underarms, or the backs of your knees. You could even use the LoveSkills technique to build your partner's sexual repertoire by asking him to stimulate you with part of his body *other* than his hands and fingers: his mouth, tongue, penis, testicles, hair—even his eyelashes. (The sensation of eyelashes barely brushing your nipples can be very arousing!)

If you feel compelled to reach out and touch your lover, or to make love to his body in some way while he is stimulating you, by all means, do so. Just as your partner is motivated by your pleasure, you can surely be turned on by his. But be sure that any overtures you initiate spring from a desire to please yourself—not your lover. The goal of this program is your sexual liberation. The Five Steps will only have the full effect if you make your satisfaction a priority.

If you have succeeded in giving your partner the LoveSkills Makeover, you are ready to move on to the next chapter.

If, on the other hand, he has resisted your attempts to teach him how to please you, read my suggestions for taming the male ego, page 81, then proceed with the next step of the program. The PowerTease Method you will learn in chapter 5 is even stronger than the LoveSkills Makeover—and it will get your man so turned on that he'll do virtually anything you want in bed.

All Play and No Work . . . can and will make you a sexually satisfied woman! If the LoveSkills training has been successful, you've already learned that sex doesn't have to be the same old grind—not for the couple who lays together and plays together.

The road to sexual satisfaction is an avenue to exploration, adventure, and greater sexual pleasure than you have ever dreamed possible. You've already taken the first steps—and there's more fun ahead. Enjoy!

5 ～

The PowerTease Method: How to Get Your Man So Turned On He'll Do Anything You Want

～

If you truly love him, the man in your life is the man of your dreams. But who is the man *in* your dreams— the magical paramour who materializes in your mind at a moment's notice to play out your wildest fantasies?

If you are like most women, the man in your dreams is not the guy who grunts at you from the other side of the breakfast table. He is probably not even a man you know. Sure, you may know his face from a movie screen or his name from a magazine story, but all you really know about your fantasy man is what he does for you— how he functions to enhance your sexuality.

Does your imaginary man leap into your bedroom only when real lovemaking is in progress? If so, you may have created him as a counterpoint to a love life that has grown dull or routine. Does he entice you to unreal heights of passion when you are alone? That's because he *is* unreal—without the moods, demands, and emotional baggage that are part and parcel of very real, very fallible men. Is he receptive to your every sexual longing, spoken and unspoken? Absolutely! Your secret desires gave him life! He is an idea you create and control. If he weren't able to please you sexually, there would be no reason for him to exist.

So what's the man in your dreams got that your real-life lover hasn't? Mystery. Excitement. Knowledge of your most intimate sexual secrets. And the willingness to take your direction, follow your lead, and satisfy you every time.

Now I'd like you to imagine something for a moment. Imagine that you have the man of your sexual dreams all alone in your bedroom. Imagine him sitting in a chair or on the edge of the bed with you standing in front of him. You are both undressed. He is yours for the taking, and he will allow you to take him to the sexual destination of your choosing, no holds barred. What would you do with him? How would you use his hands, mouth, tongue and penis to make yourself feel good? How would you take control of his body to bring more pleasure to yours?

Now, quickly, substitute your current lover for the idealized man in your fantasy. Do your plans fall flat? Are you feeling let down? Disappointed? Sexually frustrated? Wouldn't you rather be living out your fantasies with the man you love? You can—and you will.

In the previous chapter, you taught your lover how to touch, stroke, and tantalize every inch of your body so that—together—you could explore the physical aspects of making love. In this chapter, which focuses on the emotional aspects of physical intimacy, you will re-create the mystery and excitement of your sexual fantasies—and get your partner so turned on in the process he'll do anything to satisfy you!

The Name of the Game . . . is fun! The PowerTease
Method is just that—a powerful method for getting
your man to fulfill your every erotic whim, just like the
perfect lover who spices up your sexual dreams.

Of course, a sexual tease can take many forms. It can
be as subtle as a whisper. (Don't believe me? Try whis-
pering to your partner in the middle of a crowded restaurant that you are wearing no underwear and see
what happens!) It can be as overt as exposing your
breasts to him in the empty coat-check room of a night
club.

The PowerTease Method is a seduction technique
that rewards your partner for delaying his sexual gratification while encouraging him to indulge yours. Because its success hinges on your lover's willingness to
play along with a fantasy created and controlled by you,
it is important that you maintain a tone of gentle, playful titillation. To keep the sex play light, I present the
Master Hypnotist Game, a nonthreatening guided fantasy that enables you to cast your spell, become the ultimate tease, and take your pleasure, all without
threatening your partner's male ego. Play this game one
night and I guarantee your partner will be hot, bothered, bewitched—and begging for a rematch.

THE MASTER HYPNOTIST GAME

Pick a night or an afternoon when you and your
partner have lots of time to make love and you feel secure enough to introduce him to a new kind of sexual
adventure. When he has settled comfortably into the
bedroom, or when you are engaged in foreplay, begin by
saying: "Let's play a game. Let's pretend that I'm the

Master Hypnotist, and I want to put you under my spell. Once I have you in my power, I'm going to get you so excited you won't know what to do."

These can be challenging words to a man. If your husband is part of the overwhelming majority of men and welcomes your advances, you can proceed with the game. If, on the other hand, your partner is headstrong, if he is bewildered by this sudden turn of events or one of those rare men who prefers to do all the sexual initiating, he may ignore what you're saying, laugh uncomfortably, or do something to assert his masculinity, like hold you very tightly. In that case, soothe him by saying something like: "Honey, it's just a game. I'm not trying to control your life. I'm not saying we have to do this every night or every time we make love. I'm only suggesting we do this tonight. Trust me. If you relax, I know you will have a lot of fun with this, and it will really turn you on. I know it will *definitely* turn me on. You want that, don't you?"

Once he understands that this is only a game, that you're not trying to control his life outside the bedroom, that you're not going to do this every time you make love, he will most likely relax and allow you to proceed, with visions of pleasure to come dancing in his head. However, as you begin the game, keep this in mind:

PowerTeasing Step 1: Be a Loving Director—Not a Sexual Dictator.

Begin the guided fantasy by putting yourself physically in a position of control, standing near him or kneeling above him. Then set the scene just as you want it with a sexually explicit speech such as this one:

I'm the Master Hypnotist, and I'm going to put you under my spell. I want you to be sitting on the edge of the bed, naked, while I stand in front of you and slowly remove every bit of my clothing. For starters, you can look at my body, but you can't touch it. When I walk closer to you, I want you to reach out and touch my breasts and fondle my nipples, but only for a moment. Once you get my nipples erect, I'm going to take away my breasts and you can only look at them. Remember, you know my body, and you know how I like to be touched, so I want you to do it right—the way I like it most.

Remember: this is your fantasy, being brought to life. At this point you may continue to talk it through, or begin to act it out—whichever makes you feel more comfortable—and more stimulated:

Now I'll walk even closer to you, and I'll let you kiss my vagina, but only for a minute—then I'll take it away. I'm going to stand there, a couple of inches in front of you, and while I do, I'm going to touch myself and let you watch. And when I'm through, you're going to want me badly. In fact, you're going to want me so much that you'll be willing to *beg* for just a taste of what I've got.

If he balks at this last statement—or becomes put off at all—touch him on the shoulder to bring him back to reality, then calm him down with a loving reminder: "Remember, honey, this is just a game, and it's just for tonight. I'm really getting turned on by this, and we're just playing, so let me have my fun just this once." By now, he has certainly become aroused. He may even have an erection to contend with. In either case, he isn't likely to put up much resistance. As soon as he is feeling secure, continue this phase in a playful, loving, gentle, and nonthreatening way. Or move on to:

PowerTeasing Step 2: Tease Your Partner Like Crazy!!!

Give him what he wants, then after a tantalizing taste, take it away. Let him suckle your breast, then gently pull back saying, "No, no, no—not now; you've got to want it *so* badly." Allow him to stimulate your clitoris with the head of his penis, then stop short of intercourse, saying, "Uh-uh, you can't have it. You're just not turned on enough. I want you to get so hungry for me that you're ready to beg. I'll just stay here like this until I think you're turned on enough to handle it." Then underscore your request with an additional physical tease.

Virtually every woman knows what it's like to literally ache with longing—for a partner who playfully withdraws his penis at a crucial moment, for the orgasm that has been on the brink of explosion an exquisite minute too long. This is the kind of feeling you want to inspire in your partner—an insatiable hunger that is never quite satisfied; a burning need that is kindled and rekindled until his passion for you is hotter than ever before.

Knowledge is power, and nobody knows the secrets of your man's body better than you do. If he's a breast man, hold his head to your chest and playfully, teasingly wiggle your breasts in his face until your nipples stand at attention—then take them away. If he's always been attracted to your bottom, let him run his hands over its contours—then move away, giving him a bird's-eye view of what he's missing.

Don't! . . . *Stop!* . . . *Don't Stop!* . . . At this stage of the game, you may be inspired to make love—or your partner may become so excited that he tries to initiate intercourse. I encourage you, though, to try to stay true to the rules. Good things take time, and delayed sexual gratification allows arousal to build. By giving in to intercourse too soon, you may be cheating yourself—and your partner—of the opportunity to engage in some four-alarm sex. So take a step back, take a deep breath, and take a firmer hold of the controls. Tell your man that he can't touch you or stimulate you in any way until you tell him he can. Better yet, set your clock alarm for five minutes beyond the current time, then with him sitting on the edge of the bed, announce that you're going to masturbate yourself right in front of him until the alarm goes off. Because you control the pressure and the type of stimulation you're getting, this technique may enable you to delay your own orgasm—at least until the alarm goes off. After that, he can touch or kiss or do whatever he wants, and my prediction is you both will "go off" shortly thereafter.

Let your imagination run wild with this scenario, but take the physical aspects of it slow and easy. Most men find it incredibly stimulating. Combined with the element of surprise and the green light/red light nature of the tease, you'll find that you won't have to work very hard before your partner is literally panting for satisfaction. Then all you have to do is . . .

PowerTeasing Step 3: Get Your Partner So Turned on He Will Do Anything You Want.

"I'll do anything!" "Just tell me what you want!" "Please!" Hear these words during the PowerTease Method and you can be sure you've gotten your man exactly where you want him. You can also be certain there's no place on earth he'd rather be than in your bedroom, where he would gladly sell his soul (but not his body!) for your total satisfaction.

Of course, your lover doesn't have to say a thing for you to know that he is giving it up, big time, for you. If he is literally wild with passion, if he's not thinking about what he's doing in bed, just *doing*, you can be sure that he has tossed his inhibitions—and his ego— aside as eagerly as he did his clothes. In his frenzy, he may grab you or, in keeping with the spirit of the game, verbally suggest intercourse, but you should try to resist. Say something like, "Sorry, sweetheart. Tonight we're playing my game, and it's not quite over yet."

But success—especially sexual success—goes hand in hand with some intriguing dilemmas. Now that you've won his compliance, your biggest quandary may be figuring out what to do with him. Indeed, what do you do with a man who is so turned on he will do *anything* you want?

You still have two terrific techniques left in your bag of erotic tricks. And since nothing whips up a consuming passion like delaying consummation, I suggest you play this game out with one more enticing blitz.

Tease Him with the Possibility of Orgasm. By now, your lover is looking forward to his ultimate release the way a parched man searches the horizon for a desert oasis.

In his tremendously excited state he has gone some "hard miles" in the hope of satisfying his urgent needs. What you want him to do now is go the distance you need to get your pleasure as well.

In the previous chapter you taught him where and how to touch you to bring you to ecstasy. Now that you have him in your power, you can ask him to review what he's learned—and teach him a few new lessons in the process.

Let's say you've decided that what would please you most would be to have him perform oral sex on you for as long as you liked. Since you are still the Master Hypnotist (and becoming more of a master every minute!), set the scene by instructing your partner to lie on the bed on his back (so you can position yourself on top of him) or his side. Then lie down with your face and hands tantalizingly near his penis.

Tell him, "I know you're ready to come. It excites me to see your penis so big, so hard, and so ready. I'd love to see you reach your climax, to hear you gasp, or groan, or even scream with pleasure, but there's just one more little thing that needs to be taken care of first. You'll have to lick my clitoris until I'm ready to put that nice, hard penis of yours to use."

Because your mouth and hands are this close to his genitals, and because your man is closer than close to orgasm, he will give your request all he's got, hoping you'll return the favor. But you will not. Instead, you will continue the tease by using your hair to tickle the head of his penis . . . or run your tongue just once up its length . . . or kiss and lick his inner thighs without touching his penis at all. What he will get is the thrill of watching your pleasure. You, meanwhile, will have exactly what you want: prolonged oral sex.

If intercourse is more your cup of tea (or tease!), consider this alternative to the alarm-clock technique we used before. Set the alarm to go off several minutes beyond the current time. Then tell your lover that until the alarm sounds, he can insert only the tip of his penis in your vagina. Thereafter, anything goes. You'll tease yourself at the same time you're teasing him! And if you use a clock radio set to a station that plays sexy or romantic music, you'll have suitable accompaniment for whatever follows—even if what follows is one last tease:

Tease Him with Your Voice. Your voice is a powerful instrument for seduction. Depending on what you say and how you say it, your voice can carry a potent message about your sexuality—and pack an erotic punch that leaves your lover speechless.

Words create images—and images create fantasies! When you describe your sexual imaginings for your partner, or when you give him an active role in the sensual scenarios that turn you on ("I am the Master Hypnotist, and I want you to kiss my breasts like you're never going to see them again!"), you paint him into a tantalizing pleasurescape he can explore and enjoy. And when you describe what you intend to do to him ("I'm going to put my lips together and blow hot air on your penis."), then deny him, you set into motion a full-scale erotic adventure filled with so many dazzling plot twists and electrifying special effects your man can only guess at the surprise ending.

If you haven't done so before, now is the time to turn your lover on with some strong, direct sex talk—including four-letter words, if you're comfortable with them. Substitute street terms for your breasts, vagina, clitoris, and buttocks, and his penis and testicles. Use highly charged euphemisms for intercourse, oral sex, and anal sex. I guarantee that expanding your vocabulary will raise the temperature for *both* of you.

Begin now, too, to experiment with the tone, timbre, and force of your voice, using it to convey a range of emotions and moods. Enchant your lover with a softly seductive message ("Oh, I can't wait to feel you inside me.") then follow with a strong, wanton demand ("Suck my nipples. Harder!").

If you need to loosen up, or if you aren't accustomed to talking during sex, practice when you are alone in front of a mirror. Say the things you have always wanted to say during lovemaking, in your most erotic, sexy voice. Then play the temptress and the teaser while you rehearse telling your lover how to turn you on. As you increase your demands, turn up the force of your voice until you are actually giving orders—but always in a loving, playful way.

Your voice is the most versatile sex toy you can add to your collection. Play it for all it's worth! Use it to soothe, seduce, goad, challenge, control, or charmingly condescend and you'll keep your partner on his toes all the way through the final stages of this game. To keep the element of surprise in the tease, use your voice to convey the endless variety of your emotions: intense desire ("Kiss me, now!"); playful disapproval ("You call that a kiss?"); mischief ("Why are you so excited? Why is your penis so erect?"); sensuality ("Mmmm . . . that's the way I like it."); innocence ("I'd love to touch you there and make you feel really good, but I've never done that before. You'll have to show me how."); confidence ("Lick me here—and do it like you mean it.");

strength ("That's enough for now. Take your hands away and don't do it anymore.").

Getting into someone else's fantasy can be like jumping aboard a moving airplane. By varying the tone of your voice to fit the mood of the lovemaking, you will help your partner make the transition from his fantasy of the way the encounter will unfold to yours. You will also learn how to stimulate your lover to the brink of orgasm with just your voice alone, but be forewarned: this "oral sex" is potent stuff! You may be so aroused by your own erotic sound track that you may be inspired to end the game and get on with the full body contact. No problem. Your partner is certainly up to it! Just be sure to bear this final rule in mind. . . .

PowerTeasing Step 4: In the End, Always Give Your Partner What He Wants.

You can tease your partner from here to eternity and drive him crazy with passion, but before your lovemaking ends you must "deliver the goods."

Unless your partner truly enjoys being teased without consummation, or unless you are both playing a teasing game that extends beyond a single sexual encounter, it would be cruel to withhold pleasure from him through the entire session. Besides, by now, you undoubtedly aren't the model of sexual forbearance, either. If you have been sexually dissatisfied, especially if you've been unfulfilled for some time, you may feel you've delayed mutually enjoyable gratification long enough. You've already taught your lover how to touch you for maximum pleasure, so by all means fall into each other's arms! Whether you're into intercourse or opt for oral gratification, I guarantee the encounter will be the hottest ever.

Your man will probably ask for a rematch even before he's fully recovered from this first tantalizing bout with the assertive new you! To make sure he does, leave a little unfinished business from this encounter to pique his interest for the next. For example, if he loves simultaneous oral sex, put that tidbit aside for next time. It will serve as a good entrée to the next lovemaking session.

Taking Your Show on the Road. Above all, don't restrict PowerTeasing to the bedroom. A little enticement during the day is a great way to keep your partner invested in this sexual program—or prepare him for an evening of sexual fireworks. Here are some ideas for teasing your partner wherever he may be: at work, in the car or, perhaps most titillating, in public. Use them to jump-start your relationship with a resistant or indifferent lover, or come up with your own creative variations to keep the sexual momentum going between you and your partner:

- Make an erotic phone call to your partner at work—or leave a suggestive note in his briefcase, wallet, or coat pocket.

- While out driving with your partner, preferably on a deserted country road, take off your top and expose your breasts to him.

- Just before your partner comes home from work, remove your clothing and arrange the garments in a sexy trail from the front door to the bedroom.

Let your lover find you in bed, naked under the sheets.

- Serve dinner in just your panties one night. Shake your breasts at him during the meal. Dip your breasts in the dessert—chocolate mousse, whipped cream, frozen yogurt—and let him lick it off. Or rub the dessert all over your breasts and have him eat it from there.

- If you normally dress conservatively and always wear a bra, surprise your partner by wearing a dress so sheer or low-cut that no bra is possible underneath.

- Get dressed for an evening out but leave your underwear at home. Describe your situation by writing it out, in lipstick, on a cocktail napkin, then pass the message to your unsuspecting partner over drinks.

- An intimate table for two can lead to terrific intimacy. During the meal, caress your partner's knee, stroke the inside of his thigh, then slide your hand onto his penis.

- While the two of you are out in a public place (supermarket, department store, quiet hotel lobby, etc.), and when no one is looking, expose a part of your body to him by raising your dress, leaning over a table, or crossing your legs à la Sharon Stone.

- In a darkened movie theater or concert hall, rest your hand in your partner's lap and leave it there until the lights go on (in his head!).

- Whisper sexy things in his ear when you're out socially. Spice up a sedate evening by quietly suggesting something like, "What would you think if, as soon as we got in the car, I slowly took off all of my clothes until, by the time we got home, I was completely naked? And what would you do if I asked you to get in the back seat with me and rub your penis against my nipples until they got really, really hard?" Then, having given your partner something to think about, move nonchalantly over to the bar, or engage someone else in conversation.

- Have your partner take pictures of you in suggestive poses. Or take them yourself using a camera with an automatic shutter release. Put one in an envelope and tape it to the steering wheel of his car (or anywhere else he'll find it first!).

- Videotape your lovemaking. Watch it together afterwards, or just before your lover is expected home, turn on the VCR, dim the lights and wait, scantily dressed, in an unexpected place for him to find you. (One inventive woman gave a new meaning to "tool time": she let her husband find her in the home workshop, where she was relaxing nude in the wheelbarrow!)

The Power Behind PowerTeasing. As you've already seen for yourself, the PowerTease Method is a surefire technique for prolonging excitement and extending lovemaking. What you may not realize yet is that the ongoing benefits are more lasting and more transformational than any one sexual encounter could ever be.

According to the hundreds of women who have followed my Five-Step Program, this breakthrough method not only changed the way they made love but the way they experienced love—every day—with the men who share their lives. What will the PowerTease Method do for you?

1. *Make sex hot, steamy, and wild.* It will banish boredom from your bedroom forever!

2. *Reestablish intimacy and communication.* Great sex requires great honesty, and the PowerTease Method is an intensely pleasurable way to break down any barriers keeping you and the man you love apart. One seminar "graduate" described the process this way: "The first time we played the Master Hypnotist Game, my husband seemed taken aback—and more silent than ever. But two days later he took me by surprise by suggesting that we play 'my game' again, but this time he wanted to incorporate some suggestions of his own! The next thing we knew, we were discussing what turns each other on—for the first time in years!"

3. *Give you all the time you need to get all the pleasure you can.* Because you control how, when, and to what extent you are stimulated, the PowerTease Method puts an end to the "get naked, get busy, get off" kind of sex that leaves most women frustrated.

4. *Encourage your partner to invest in your quest for sexual satisfaction.* He may believe that a man is the king of his castle, but, in the bedroom, the penis rules! His obvious excitement is tangible proof that there is much to be gained by letting up on the machismo.

PowerTeasing is a uniquely pleasurable route to a man's sexual enlightenment. For many women I know it has been a real catalyst for change—between the sheets and between committed partners. Don't be surprised if your man develops a sensitivity that extends to other areas of your life as well. And, most of all:

5. *The PowerTease Method provides a safe foundation upon which you can build—and live out—your sexual dreams.* In many ways, our erotic fantasies are the most private of our private parts. Locked away in our minds, they are untouched—untouchable—and so long as they remain there, they will remain unfulfilled.

Yet to benefit from the PowerTease Method it really doesn't matter whether you become the Master Hypnotist or not. You can substitute a more personal scenario—or decide not to use a fantasy at all. Simply by demanding the pleasure you know you deserve, you bring to life one of a woman's most arousing erotic dreams: the fantasy of the sexual adventurer—free to explore and exceed the outermost limits of untamed desire. And although you may not have realized it, that role is not new to you. The sexual adventurer has always been deep within you—a fantasy waiting to be realized.

For men and women alike, erotic dreams are the key to sexual liberation. If you have been successful with the program so far, you are already beginning to see how fantasy-sharing and role-playing will work to unlock the sexual psyche and set your deepest passions free. In the chapters to come, you will awaken all the women you are in your wildest imaginings: the temptress, the vixen, the captive, the siren, the demure lover. In short, you will become a sexually satisfied woman.

6 ∾

The Wild Night Experience: How to Tame the Macho Man in Your Man

∾

If your erotic fantasies have been more exciting than connubial reality; if an active, happy sex life has been the missing link in your relationship; if you have been sexually dissatisfied in any way, for any length of time, then Wild Night is what you've been waiting for! An opportunity to celebrate the full animal nature of your sexuality, Wild Night is a sexual coming-out party at which you can proudly debut all the new skills you've learned in this program. In a very real sense, Wild Night is also a coming-in party. Wild Nighttime is the right time to pull your lover into the heart of your erotic journey and make him a full partner in your quest for sexual satisfaction.

However powerful his urge to control the action in the erotic arena, no matter how one-sided your intimate relationship has been in the past, if you have followed my Five-Step Program up to this point, you have already learned to pleasure and tease your man into submission—and he has learned that, at least between the sheets, submission can have *very* palpable rewards. Three cheers for you! Through your "naked ambition," you have laid the foundation for opening yourself fully to your partner, discovering who you are sexually, and bringing your erotic dreams to life.

But if your lover has resisted your attempts to change the way you make love, if his need to overpower and control seems stronger than his desire for passion and intimacy, then he has become the proverbial wet blanket in your bedroom—and an actual barrier to your sexual liberation.

Great sex is an ongoing adventure—a journey without limits, without inhibitions, without end. With a resistant partner in tow, however, the road ahead can simply seem, well, endless. First of all, it is difficult to achieve true passion with a partner who is fighting you all the way. Lovemaking is always frustrating when it is defined by your partner's limitations. Second, it is impossible to express your deepest desires to a partner who is not interested in or invested in your sexual pleasure. If he turns off on your sexual needs, it is only a matter of time before all intimacy shuts down entirely.

Theoretically, it is possible for you to work through this entire program without your partner's cooperation and still achieve a measure of sexual satisfaction. You can unlock your sexuality whether your partner wants to join you or not. But that would be a hollow victory. The goal of Wild Night is not to overcome your partner or threaten his masculinity but to overwhelm him with pleasure, to reward him for "giving up" control, and to free him to pursue any and every avenue that leads you both to sexual satisfaction. That means liberating his libido—and his masculine ego as well.

Understanding the Macho in the Man. As a topic, the male ego could fill a book of its own. As an inhibitor to sexual satisfaction, the self-centered, self-protective male ego can fill your life with frustration, anger, resentment, feelings of isolation, and a nagging sense of inferiority or even insignificance.

Of course, there is nothing inherently unhealthy about ego. A healthy ego allows you to give without feeling like a martyr; it permits you to take without feeling selfish or guilty. In short, a hale and hearty ego is what empowers you to ask for and get what you want in bed! It is only when ego becomes egocentric—that is, self-serving to the exclusion of the needs of others—that it becomes a self-protective device—and a barrier to sexual exploration of any kind.

Where does the prideful, stubborn, emotionally remote behavior we know as the unhealthy male ego come from? One woman I know swears that "mucho macho" is the direct result of testosterone overload, and to some extent, she may be right. As politically incorrect as it sounds, modern researchers assert that young males are more physically inclined—and, as a result, more aggressive, territorial, and controlling—than their female counterparts. Of course, it is debatable whether adult men really stake out four-bedroom suburban homes as turf or insist on calling the shots in those bedrooms because they are "hormonally challenged." What is certain is that these self-defeating behaviors have been bred into men since *Australopithecus* loped across the earth and uttered (with remarkable panache) "Ugh."

Macho behavior appears to have begun as a day-to-day survival mechanism. Some scientists claim that early man closed off his emotions to increase his awareness of dangers lurking nearby. When he bonded with a mate, he took his cue from his larger, stronger physique. He became her protector—and she became his property. And when they had offspring, he became the prehistoric breadwinner. He competed with other males for food, pitting his stubborn strength against fierce animals. It was either bring home the bacon or become it.

Men have long since traded in their loin cloths and spears for Armani suits and briefcases, but it isn't difficult to see how little those roles have changed in a few million years. Most men still close off their softer emotions or mask their vulnerability with an impenetrable masculine veneer in order to defend themselves from possible pain. Some take it upon themselves to protect the women they love from any potential threat (including the danger of "uncontrollable" female sexuality). And although the male ego is a survival mechanism that, in many ways, has outsurvived its usefulness, men continue to compete: in sports, in business—and in the most high-risk milieu of all, the sexual arena.

You Can Take the Man out of the Cave, but . . . Emily was a twenty-seven-year-old woman who enrolled in my seminar. Although the discussion was always lively, Emily didn't participate until the topic turned to the male ego. Then she took the group by storm.

"My boyfriend, Tom, literally swept me off my feet," she told us. "Within minutes of meeting him at a party, he simply picked me up, threw me over his shoulder, and headed for the door. On the way out, he said to the hostess, 'Okay, I've found what I was looking for. There's no use hanging around here any longer!'

"I probably don't have to tell the women in the room I was flattered out of my mind! Here was this strong, handsome renegade who wanted me so badly he took me captive in front of a whole roomful of people! For nearly a year, I didn't care whether or not he could put two words together to make a sentence. I didn't care that he was too jealous to allow me to see my old friends. I didn't even care that sex was an all-or-nothing proposition—meaning all for him and nothing for me. He was mysterious, protective, primal. . . .

"Four years later, he doesn't seem so mysterious and protective to me anymore—just emotionally repressed and pitifully insecure. And as for sex . . . it's still all or nothing. But I've opted for the nothing."

Traditional values die hard, especially in a society that rewards 50 percent of its citizens for their compliance, sexual passivity, and powerlessness. Can it really surprise us that so many women are still swept away by a man's physical strength, raw courage, stoicism, skill in battle, competence in the world, and mastery of women? It shouldn't. In business courses and James Bond movies, in professional sports and romance novels, these chest-pounding characteristics are the mark of a man who will conquer the world. Since these behaviors are discouraged in women, the only way the female of the species can acceptably acquire success is vicariously—through a hard-driving, hard-headed man.

What does all this have to do with your struggle to achieve sexual satisfaction? It's simple. If you take a traditional man steeped in traditional male values and point him toward the bedroom door, he will view lovemaking as another of his competitive sports. Using only tried-and-true methods (experimentation can fail, you know, and who wants a blot like *that* on his scorecard?), he will work toward his perceived mission: maintaining his erection until he satisfies you in some basic way. For your benefit he may dabble in foreplay, but even while he's performing cunnilingus or stroking you, he lets you know that the clock is ticking. For him, the real game doesn't start until intercourse begins. That's when he can allow himself to "score"—and congratulate himself on his command performance. It's no secret that that sort of perfunctory sex is frustrating for a woman. What *is* a secret, however, is how ambivalent men really are about the traditional roles they play—particularly in bed.

Secrets Your Lover Never Told You. Although he may not be conscious of it, every man knows in his heart that masculine posturing is a defense mechanism that distances him from a full rollicking enjoyment of sex. And although he may never admit it, *your* man harbors a secret desire that you will do for him what he cannot: break the confines of his male ego; become the sexual aggressor; and pull him, kicking and howling with pleasure, into an ongoing sexual adventure that will curl the hair on his chest.

Ask him and he may deny it; confront him and he may resist it, but the fact that a man secretly *wants* a woman to take control in bed is well documented in research. In conducting research for my first book, *How to Save Your Marriage from an Affair,* I found that men who have affairs almost always seek out women who are sexually aggressive. A book of sexual surveys published in 1991, *Do You Do It with the Lights On?,* showed that 91 percent of the men surveyed (98 percent of men aged thirty to fifty-four!) not only wanted their mates to be more aggressive during lovemaking, they wanted them to choose the position, the place, and the procedure. In addition, a surprisingly large number of men harbor a desire for their women to "order them around" in bed. In fact, the practice of sexual dominance by women is legendary in places like the United Kingdom, where men are known for their stiff upper lips.

As always, the goal of this book is to get *you* to take control of your erotic destiny—and that means developing a lighthearted sense of sexual assertiveness that works as a psychological aphrodisiac for both you and your partner. Wild Night is an erotic one-act play with a climactic ending. Its theme is that when it comes to your fulfillment, you aren't taking male dominance lying down anymore! It is also an extraordinarily direct and powerful way to put your partner's performance anxieties to rest so he can play out all of his secret fantasies.

Preparing Your Partner for Wild Night. Wild Night has the potential to be the most electric, memorable, and transformational sexual experience of your life. Depending on how deeply entrenched your lover is in ego-based behavior, Wild Night could also be panic time for him. Control isn't an easy thing to give up—or even to share. For many men, wearing the pants in the family is a point of honor, a source of power, and—second to the proud ownership of a penis—an indisputable proof of masculine identity. Your mission here is to show your lover that getting out of his pants can be more rewarding than wielding dominance.

The following techniques are a form of foreplay designed to prepare your partner for the wildest night of his life. Use them on the sexually adventurous man and they will make the transition to fantasy-based sex even smoother. Try them on the resistant lover and he will gladly trade in his obsolete need for control on a spanking new desire for pleasure—and that will ensure that sex is *always* a pleasure for you.

Preliminary Technique 1: The Body Language of Love

Ancient man got one thing right: the male ego gets soft when the penis is not! When you're in bed making love with your partner, especially during foreplay, observe his body language and take note of any physical signs that he has relaxed his defenses. If he is making love to you with his eyes tightly shut, if his mind is on his work rather than his companion, he is probably deep into "performance mode"—and he won't want to be interrupted with any new ideas. If, on the other hand, his eyes are wide with pleasure, or if he is simply lying back and allowing himself to enjoy the way you are pleasuring him, then the proverbial iron is hot and it's time to strike.

Issue a loving and playful invitation to the joys of sharing control. Say something like, "Honey, how would you like me to be a little more aggressive with you tonight? I'd love to tell you some of the things that I'd like you to do to me." If he says yes, pick up on some of the tantalizing activities you never got to during the Master Hypnotist Game. Be direct and explicit about what you want ("Get on your back so I can climb on top of you."), but keep your tone and delivery light. If he wavers, or is unsure when you ask him if he wants you to be aggressive, go ahead and try it anyway. He may be looking for permission—or dealing with some inhibitions of his own.

If your man refuses to allow you to take the sexual reins for now, wait for the next opportune moment:

right after his orgasm. At that point he is relaxed and his defenses are down, even if the sex act *was* a performance for him. Of course, he may want to roll over and go to sleep, but if you stroke his body a little bit to reinforce the idea that you only want to bring him physical pleasure, he will tune in to your message. Whisper lovingly, "Honey, I'd like to be aggressive with you some night, and tell you some naughty things I'd like you to do with me. What do you think? Would you like that?" He may be intrigued enough to give in, or he may agree just to humor you. It really doesn't matter. Any "yes" can be pounced on next time, so take him at his word. And if he still resists? Take him by surprise!

Preliminary Technique 2: Ambushing the Ambivalent Man

Some of the wildest Wild Nights I've heard about have begun during the day! And why not? When the sun is shining, the birds are singing, and your man's sexual guard is down, a little unexpected aggression on your part may come as an extremely pleasurable surprise. How to set a trap for your macho man? Try some of these ideas.

- When he comes home from work, stand in the doorway dressed in sexy lingerie. Pose with one arm on the door jamb and your other hand on your hip to give the scene a bordello look and say, "Welcome to my cathouse, mister. You'd better be ready for what I have in store for you."

- When *you* come home from work, rush in the door, toss your briefcase aside and, before your lover has a chance to catch his breath, corner him wherever he is and perform oral sex on him. Or tease him by stopping halfway through and say, "If you want more of that you'd better come with me. . . ."

- While you are occupied with a chore or activity, turn suddenly in your lover's direction and start undoing his pants. If he responds with embarrassment or seems uptight and rigid, he may be worried that you want to have sex with him then and there—and fearful that he (or his penis!) might fall short under pressure. Continue to stroke him gently, then reassure him by telling him, "I don't want to have intercourse right now. All I want to do is turn you on. You don't have to do anything except stand here, let yourself go—and enjoy what I can do for you." Bring him to an orgasm if you like, then walk away nonchalantly.

  Later, when he whispers his pleasure in your ear, take the opportunity to tease him a little. Ask him, "Wouldn't you like me to be more aggressive like that in bed? I'd love to be able to tell you how to please me—how to make me come." Since you've already shown him what's in it for him, it's an offer few men could refuse.

- When he least expects it, tickle him through the front of his pants. Playfully grab him and tease him there. Say: "What's this? Huh? What *is* this thing? I really feel something here. Could it be getting bigger? Wow, look at that! Let's see if I can turn you on. How does that feel? Huh? Let's see how far we can go with this. Do you think we can go all the way?" If he laughs at your overture, laugh with him! A good giggle is the best medicine for the seriousness of the male ego. The scenario will turn sensual soon enough. When it does, bring him to an orgasm if you like, and then walk away mischievously.

• If he is doing that armchair athlete thing, stride into the living room, take your clothes off in a no-nonsense way, climb on top of him and announce, "I want some. *Now!*" Sit on his lap, facing him, then reach down with one hand and grab his penis. Then run the other hand through his hair and tug his head back just a little while you get in his face and say, "I'm going to make you do all those naughty things you've been wanting to do your whole life." If he retorts, "Oh, yeah? Like what?", challenge him to reveal his fantasies. Say: "That's just what I'm going to find out. Now tell me what they are, one at a time." No man is going to let a power struggle stand in the way of his ultimate pleasure! Once you've let your man know that you're willing to act on his desires, he'll be willing to give you all the leeway you need. He'll also be primed and ready to move on to the main event— the first of many wild nights!

WILD NIGHT

Wild Night is the unforgettable night you will actually become every man's fantasy—and fulfill your own need for sexual self-determination at the same time. It is your opportunity to pull out all the stops, to take on an exciting new role filled with undiscovered pleasures and turn your bed into a magical stage on which you can play out all of your deepest desires—for your partner's pleasure and your own.

At first glance, it may seem that Wild Night promises to be everything to everybody, but there are a few things this special evening is not. First of all, Wild Night is not an exercise in fantasy-sharing (the subject of chapter 7). It is a game based on a generic or commonly held fantasy. To get the most out of Wild Night, you need share none of your most intimate thoughts or desires. Second, although Wild Night requires you to dress for success in the boudoir, it is not the same as sexual play-acting (the subject of chapter 8). Play-acting is a specific technique designed to bring your personal fantasies—rather than commonly held desires—to life. Finally, Wild Night is anything *but* good, clean fun. It is a down-and-dirty delight enabling you to feel your sexual oats, enjoy power as an aphrodisiac, and hit your partner where it matters most: right in his deep-seated desire to be ravished by a woman who is beyond his control—in ways that are beyond his imagination.

The Three Steps. Although Wild Night has every characteristic of a great one-act play—mystery, intrigue, titillation, a theme, even a climactic ending—it requires only three simple steps:

1. Setting the Scene
2. The Call of the Wild
3. Acting the Part

Since the first and second steps flow naturally into each other (as you and your partner will!) I will explain them together.

In this game of let's pretend, you will physically enact a common sexual fantasy—the fantasy of the sexually aggressive woman—using clothing, accessories, props, music, mood, lighting and anything else that will add realism and eroticism to the scene. You will also get an opportunity to "be" the woman of your sexual dreams—a sex goddess, the queen of the Amazons, a modern day Mata Hari, a rock star, or any other powerful female figure that best expresses *your* vision of the sexually liberated woman.

As in any well-crafted play, the action (and there will be plenty!), setting and theme stem from the development of the characters. Since you alone will have top billing in this Wild Night production, it is crucial that you choose a role that appeals to you, either from the sample scenarios that follow or from your own Well of Sexual Dreams.

As you make your selection, particularly if you are choosing among the cast of characters that populate your own sexual fantasies, be aware that many themes are available to erotic play-actors. Eventually you may want to explore themes like helplessness, temptation, innocence, captivity, or naïveté to stretch your scope as a sexual thespian. Since the purpose of Wild Night is to put you in full control of the action (and since adopting a passive role would leave your partner without a clue as to how to proceed), you must select a role that allows you to direct the activity in the bedroom—at least for now. These suggested vignettes may differ in plot (What It's About), atmosphere (What to Wear), and script (What to Say), but they all share a single, common theme: that *you* are the one calling the shots. Whether you follow them to the letter or use them as inspiration, I suggest that you choose a plot, appropriate dress, and a script that is faithful to the cause of your sexual self-determination.

"THE GODDESS OF THE NIGHT"

What It's About	You are a strong, confident, sexy woman—and an erotic force to be reckoned with. Your only goal is to satisfy your sexual desires and you aren't about to let any man's quibbles stand in your way.
What to Wear	Sexy lingerie—black is best—or any leather clothing you might have on hand. If your closet is bare, wear his leather jacket with black lingerie underneath . . . or nothing at all. To avoid leaving fingerprints on your hapless victim, put on black lace or leather gloves.
What to Say	"I am the Goddess of the Night and tonight you're to do what I want."

"CAT ON A HOT TIN ROOF"

What It's About	You're a sexy, high-priced prostitute with some low-down needs of her own.

What to Wear	Get on your vampiest dress and those "do-me" spike heels, Mama, because you're going to get yours to-night.
What to Say	"Hello, Big Boy. Got a problem? I'll take care of it for you. But you're going to have to take care of *me* first."

"BAD GIRLS AND NAUGHTY BOYS"

What It's About	You're a "Mistress"—an irresistible dominatrix—who must playfully teach her misbehaving partner a lesson.
What to Wear	Any of the black leather clothing listed in "The Goddess of the Night" is fair game. To play the role to the hilt, try a garter belt, leather bra, leather miniskirt, black gloves, black fishnet stockings, and the highest-heeled shoes (tall women are intimidating!) or black leather boots that reach almost to you-know-where. Wear sunglasses—preferably with reflective lenses—to minimize eye contact. (That's not the kind of contact you have in mind.) Carry an item that suggests punishment in a *very playful* way—like a feather duster.

What to Say   "Hello, young man. I am Miss
_____" (your first name), "and to-
night you will do as I say. Do you
understand?"

"WILD THING"

What It's About   You're a creature of the jungle, a
cross between a wanton Amazon
and a pleasure-seeking animal.
You've been walking through the
jungle and you've stumbled onto
your partner, who has become
caught in your trap.

What to Wear   Any kind of animal-print clothing—perhaps a dress, torn at the
bottom. (A leopard-print nightgown
will do in a pinch.) Wear no underwear. Let your bare arms show. You
can even smear them with dark eye
shadow to make it look like you've
been out pillaging in the bush. Wear
an arm band or a serpent bracelet
around your upper arm. Go heavy
on the eye liner and eye shadow.
Let your hair go really wild. Wear
press-on fingernails for extra
effect—they're great for *playful*
scratching. (No bloodletting, please!
This is not a vampire scenario.)

What to Say   "I am a tigress and I am here to satisfy my hunger. You will not escape." Or, "I am 'She.' Who dares disturb my lair?"

"ROCK ME"

What It's About   You are your partner's favorite female rock star—the one he fantasizes about to the tune of hundreds of dollars in CDs. It is after the concert, and you discover him hiding in your dressing room. Note: To bring this scenario to a crescendo, you might even encourage your lover to call you by his fantasy woman's name. Don't worry that he will fall in love with her and forget about you—he knows very well who he's getting his pleasure from! If, on the other hand, you are concerned that "she" is somehow going to wrest him out of your life, see my discussion of the same fear from the man's point of view on page 111.

What to Wear   Try to imitate the outfit she wears on his favorite album cover or video. Or drape yourself in rock-star black.

What to Say   "How did you get backstage? And
                     how did you get into my dressing
                     room? My bodyguards are supposed
                     to protect me from fans like you. On
                     the other hand, maybe I've been
                     overprotected lately. . . ." (Slink
                     down onto the bed.) "Well, now
                     that you're here, why don't you tell
                     me all the things you've been want-
                     ing to do to me since you've become
                     my number-one fan? Better yet, why
                     don't we rehearse them now?"

"SECRET AGENT"

What It's About   You're a covert agent from the Spe-
                     cial Forces, and you're in town to
                     make a very sensual contact.

What to Wear   Wear a dark business suit—
                     preferably a man's—with a white
                     shirt and dark tie, and no underwear
                     underneath. Wear a man's fedora
                     (your partner's, if he has one) and
                     perhaps sunglasses to add an extra
                     touch of secrecy. Be very business-
                     like. You might even carry a brief-
                     case into the bedroom—then open
                     it to reveal a cache of sex toys you
                     intend to use for your pleasure and
                     his.

What to Say   "Good evening, Mr. _____ " (his
               last name). "I'm a secret agent from
               the _____ (CIA, KGB, Secret
               Service, etc.), and your mission—
               should you decide to accept it—is to
               drive me wild."

Step 1: Setting the Scene.

Whether you choose to portray a swashbuckling pi-
rate and swoop down on your lover like a female Erroll
Flynn, or do it up as a 1920s gangster lady just to prove
how many ways there are to break the law, set the
scene as dramatically and realistically as you can. Hide
your costume in a convenient place so you can effect a
quick change while your unsuspecting partner settles
into bed. Or take a hint from a creative woman in my
seminar and set the stage for romance big time in a
seldom-used room. A girls'-group leader, she set up
an entire camping scene—complete with pop-up tent,
sleeping bags, foliage plants, and a tape recording of
forest sounds—in a guest bedroom, then lured her husband in on the pretext of fixing a window! While he
gaped at the transformation, she made some tantalizing
alterations to her uniform (ah, the things one can do
with a sash and a beanie!). When she finally burst in to
announce that she was his leader—and that she would
be teaching him "the right way to start a fire"—he was
more than willing to rub together any combination of
body parts to add spark to the experience.

Such a transformation takes planning, I know, but it
is certainly a rewarding endeavor. With a ten dollar
Mombasa net or an inexpensive sound-effects record,
you can effect enough of a change to transport your

man out of his dull environment and into a place where lovemaking is anything but routine. With a bathtub full of water and a handful of candles, you can immerse your lover in mystery and excitement and whet his appetite for whatever comes next. What *does* come next?

Step 2: The Call of the Wild.

Perhaps the most intriguing step in the Wild Night process, the Call of the Wild is the moment when you reveal yourself verbally to your partner; announce the presence of the character you have adopted in a compelling way; and in your most commanding, come-hither or go-thither voice, summon your lover into the tangible joys of fantasy-based lovemaking.

Remember: this step is named Call of the Wild, not Whimper of the Mild, so whatever you do, make his first impression of you as strong, as memorable, and as true to your character as possible. If you are doing that insatiable woman thing, pose in the bedroom doorway and look him up and down like you are sizing up a piece of meat. If you have opted for the secret-agent scenario, stride purposefully into the room, then playfully back your lover into a chair to intimidate him a little. Allow yourself time to get into the spirit of the scene by flirting, flaunting, or otherwise physically enacting the role you are playing. Then look him straight in the eye and tell him, in just a few sentences, who you are, what you want, and what lengths you are willing to go to to get it.

Speechless in Southern California. Marta was a bright, beautiful, and usually talkative forty-year-old woman who stopped by for a chat after a seminar meeting. "I've had a drop-dead sexy catwoman outfit set aside for weeks," she told me. "I'm dying to wear it—and I know it would turn my boyfriend, Ray, on like crazy. But I haven't used it. You see, I'm comfortable enough to play the part. . . . I just can't bring myself to *say* the part."

Nearly no one knows more about the power of words than the sexually passive woman. Steeped in the belief that no real lady "asks for it," she would rather swallow her dissatisfaction than appear too aggressive in the bedroom. Brought up to believe that sexual longing is a "bad" feeling and that words make feelings real, she feels safer dressing the part of a sexually satisfied woman than she does addressing the reality of her own desires.

I knew what Marta was really asking me: she wanted permission to play the catwoman role without uttering even a simple "meow." It was permission I could not give. In the course of my career, I had spoken to hundreds of women who tried to dress their way to sexual success. What I learned from them was that without verbal direction, Marta would simply be getting all vamped up with nowhere to go—except back to the unfulfilling habits that led her to me in the first place.

I asked Marta if she had tried to play the Master Hypnotist Game. She blushed to the roots of her hair. She admitted she had, and although her lover had initially laughed at the premise, the evening had been a smashing success. "I guess I'm a one-sentence wonder," declared Marta. "I can make it through a few choice words, but to actually play a role, stay in character, and reveal my desires—just the thought of it makes me feel . . . *naked*."

Marta was right about one thing: she indeed was a wonder. By blurting out her intentions and playing out the Master Hypnotist scenario despite her fear, she had overcome a powerful and common sexual inhibition. I told her that with just a few words and a little effort, she had taken great strides towards achieving sexual satisfaction.

I also reassured her that Wild Night would be easier than she thought. Dressing up is in itself a great communicator. By choosing a costume she was comfortable with, Marta was sure to send her lover a powerful message. If all she could manage was one sentence to set the scene, then one sentence would do—at least until she was able to reveal her emotions with the same abandon that she revealed her body.

If the idea of verbal sexplay leaves you feeling emotionally naked, remember: sex is an activity that is best enjoyed naked. Lay bare your desires, thoughts and emotions and you will greatly enhance this Wild Night as well as those to follow. If you can, follow Marta's lead and vow to express yourself a little more with each sexual experience.

Step 3: Acting the Part.

Ham it up. Vamp it up. Do whatever you have to do to shake up the status quo! You've got your partner right where you want him: front and center for the hottest display of sexual talent and erotic virtuosity this side of Easy Street! Put on some music and strut your stuff in time to his pounding heart. Let him know that you're a force to be reckoned with. Use your props in imaginative ways. (A bed, a feather duster, and thou!) No matter what he says, no matter what he does, stay

in character. Make it clear that something special is going to happen tonight, and only you know what it is.

Prowl the bed like a panther, circling its prey. Move
close enough to your lover to brush his nipples through
his shirt with your fingernails, then dance nonchalantly
away. Don't be afraid to be a little forceful with him or
let him know who's in charge of this production. Sidle
toward him with one hand on the top of your costume,
as if you mean to take it off. Then, when you're close
enough for him to get a whiff of your perfume, use that
same hand to playfully push him down onto his back.
Let him unzip your boots—then threaten to tie him up
with your scarf if he attempts to do the same with his
pants. Be wicked. Be sly. Be mischievous. Be bold!

"Attack" him at times. Jump on the bed and grab or
lick him where he least expects it—then jump off and
prowl the room again. Tickle him with a prop—a vel-
vet glove, the long hair of a wig, the toe of a spike
heel—or sensuously remove a fishnet stocking from
your garter, and run it up the length of his body.

When it's clear he'll do anything you want, be playfully demanding. Give him sexual commands he
wouldn't think to refuse. Tell him, "Grab your penis—
let me see you get excited," then stand in front of him,
legs apart, as he does. Or stand with your back to him,
plant your hands on yours hips, look over your shoulder
and say, "Kiss my buns!" Don't hesitate to tell him what
to do. This scenario is a sexual dream come true for
him, so make him yours for the evening.

If he resists in any way, put a provocative hold on
him such as this one: with him on the bed, put your leg
over him, then grab his penis underneath or behind
you. Reach up with your other hand and twine your
fingers in his hair. Then bend down and whisper in his

ear, "I want you to be *mine* tonight!" Tug at him with both hands when you say the word *mine*, just for emphasis.

Character development takes time, so don't rush your performance. Let your "personality" unfold within the framework of the natural flow of the sex play. Try out your character's most daring stunts and devices. (Certain characters, like the prostitute, are notorious for knowing every "trick" in the book!) And always respond to your partner's suggestions as your character would. (A friend of mine who made her Wild Night debut as a policewoman brushed aside all her husband's queries with a curt "request denied.") Keep him guessing, keep him interested, and keep him wanting more.

For a grand finale, break out the PowerTease Method you learned in the previous chapter. Tease your partner until he seems ready to explode with desire. Better yet, tease him as long as *you* can stand it, then consummate the evening with hot, wild sex.

Bring each other to climax any way you like—with intercourse, oral sex, or—to make this a night neither of you will forget—a sexual variation you've never explored. When it's all over but the panting, the two of you will be exhausted and happy—and bubbling over with new ideas for the next Wild Night, and the one after that, and the one after that. . . .

Wild Night may have seemed like a sexual crescendo, but it is actually an introductory game designed to prepare you for the next two stages of the Five-Step Program. An erotic blend of light fantasy-sharing and rudimentary play-acting (the subjects of chapters 7 and 8), Wild Night is the last bridge you will cross on your journey to sexual satisfaction. A bold and pleasurable transition, it is the essential link connecting all you have learned so far with the truly transformational techniques that lie ahead.

As liberating as it may have been for you, remember: Wild Night focused on *your partner's* hidden desires. The pages to come will shed light on *your* deepest sexual secrets and lead you to the culmination of your erotic dreams—when all your fantasies come vividly to life.

7 ～

Sharing Visions of Wonderland: Talking out Your Sexual Fantasies for the Fun (and Pleasure) of It

～

A sleek, black limousine moves slowly along a deserted city street. It is late. The stately stone buildings that line the street have long since gone dark. The only source of illumination on their elegant facades is the dim glow of a streetlight. The limo pulls to the curb near the streetlight and stops.

A woman steps out of the car. She is dressed in a strapless black evening dress. In one gloved hand, she clutches a small black handbag. As she steps onto the sidewalk, she is suddenly overcome with desire. Her knees grow weak, and she leans against the lamppost for support.

As wave after wave of passion overcomes her, she closes her eyes, tilts her head back, and arches her spine against the cool steel of the streetlight. The handbag drops.

She runs her hands briefly through her hair, then, with the tips of her gloved fingers, she begins to slowly trace the contours of her face, the smooth line of her neck, the peaks and hollows of her breasts, and the soft curves of her body. She moans softly; there is no one around to hear her. In response to her mounting desire, her fingers begin their urgent explorations again.

Caught up in the passion of the moment, she has lost all sense of time, place, and propriety. She begins to slide down the lamppost, slowly—very slowly—until she crumples to the ground, her head resting on her knees, her arms wrapped around her like a full-length mink. For a few moments, she becomes a part of the streetscape, as lifeless and graceful as the buildings around her. Then she opens her eyes.

Suddenly, she is aware of her surroundings. She slowly brings herself to a standing position, straightens her dress and regains her composure. She smooths her hair with her fingers, picks up her handbag, and gets back into the waiting limousine. The street is empty once again.

What you've just read is a fantasy. It was related to me by Laura, to whom I introduced you in chapter 2. The mere fact that Laura was able to create, experience, and enjoy this fantasy marked the beginning of her journey through the Wonderland of her sexual imagination. That she was ultimately able to share this vision with her partner, to use it as a springboard for their mutual pleasure, marked her transition from a lifetime of sexual dissatisfaction to a life filled with deep intimacy, mutual love and respect, and unlimited erotic possibilities.

If you've worked through the exercises, activities, and concepts in this book so far, you have already begun to explore the magical place where feelings become desires and desires take on a life of their own. In chapter 2, you learned about the fantasies you have stored in your deep and limitless Well of Sexual Dreams. You also came to see that by dipping into that well, you could refresh yourself erotically, revive your depleted libido, and revitalize your sexual nature. In chapter 4, you learned to focus your concentration on your pleasure, identify your body's hot spots, and turn the man you love into the attentive, inventive lover you've always dreamed about. Chapter 5 introduced the Power-Tease Method, a no-holds-barred technique based on a generic or universally held fantasy. And if you worked through chapter 6, you discovered how to set the night on fire by enacting a common (but uncommonly exciting!) sexual theme.

The goal of this chapter is to bring your sexual fantasies more directly into the lovemaking experience, share the transformational power of your erotic dreams with your partner, and bring you one step closer to total sexual satisfaction.

Prelude to a Shared Fantasy. The idea behind fantasy-sharing is very simple. While you're making love—enjoying intercourse, oral sex, manual stimulation, etc.—you stimulate yourself and your partner by relating explicitly a fantasy that turns you on. If, for instance, that fantasy involves you and your partner, you describe the sexual interaction, who is doing what to whom, and the way your imaginary activities make you feel. If, on the other hand, your sexual dream revolves around a detailed erotic scene, you try to paint as vivid a picture of that scene as you possibly can to bring your partner more fully into the experience.

Of course, describing your sexual fantasies is not like doing the color commentary for a professional football game. You won't be broadcasting from a booth far above the fray. You'll be venting your feelings from the middle of the sexual arena while the action is at its hottest and heaviest! Intricate plot details may emerge in breathless gasps; you may yell out salient points along with your pleasure; or you may become tongue-tied with excitement and have trouble talking at all. Certainly, if you were to make a tape of this kind of storytelling, it would not be suitable for Sunday school story hour. But it couldn't matter less how you sound. The important thing is that you use your sexual fantasies as aural aphrodisiacs, crank up the levels of pleasure in your lovemaking, and speak what is on your mind *while you are making love.*

The Joys of Fantasy-sharing. You may have "done it" while swinging from a crystal chandelier or on the back of a camel trudging across the Mojave Desert. You may have wrung pleasure from every part of your body from your eyebrows to your toenails. (Ouch!) But I am not exaggerating when I tell you that fantasy-sharing is the most intense sexual experience you will ever have the opportunity to enjoy.

Think about it. If at the heart of every fantasy is a feeling (and there is), and sharing your sexual fantasies is an arousing form of emotional release (and it is!), then fantasy-sharing during physical sex is a surefire way to arouse and satiate you—body, mind and soul!

To restate my case as unscientifically as possible: physical sex may rock the bed, but fantasy-sharing, combined with physical stimulation, will blow your mind! Expressing your deepest feelings is an emotional pleasure. Sex is a carnal pleasure. Put the two together and you have a combination that is a quantum leap be-

yond basic physical consummation—a pleasurable one–
two punch that is literally "better than sex."

Of course, getting twice the "bang" is enough to recommend any sexual technique, but the benefits of
fantasy-sharing don't stop there. Fantasy-sharing is a
true liberating force enabling you to express your
pent-up emotions, including closeted feelings you may
have harbored for many years, perhaps without even
knowing it. A proven method for airing your fantasies
and feelings, fantasy-sharing can bring about tremendous relief, a lasting sense of well-being, and a feeling
of total emancipation from the effects of long-term frustration. More than one woman who experimented with
this erotically evolved method described it as "cleans-
ing."

The women in my seminars have also reported that
fantasy-sharing is a direct route to establishing a more
honest and intimate bond with their partners—and it
is. Sharing your sexual dreams during lovemaking
means opening your mind to the man you love as readily as you do your body, at a very vulnerable moment.
When your partner accepts the fantastical products of
your imagination (and he will!), it is a sign that he accepts you unconditionally as a human being who has
thoughts and desires of her own. Certainly there is
nothing more gratifying than that! The real secret to
sexual satisfaction is now and always has been soul-
baring intimacy. No sexual technique—and absolutely
no program—can substitute for the impenetrable bond
formed by two people who are willing to open themselves fully to each other.

By now you're getting the idea that fantasy-sharing
has some serious emotional benefits, but the most pro-
found advantage of revealing your erotic dreams is that

it is fun! When you fantasize privately, when you limit scenarios that arouse you to the confines of your mind, you glimpse only a small part of your fantasy (usually only enough to masturbate, or to "put you over" in unsatisfying sexual circumstances). But when you share your fantasy out loud with your partner, it takes on a life of its own. Made real by your words, your erotic dream appears in all its richness and dimension. You can see it in its entirety, examine it from all sides, explore it with your partner like uncharted virgin territory. Your lover will be mesmerized by the beauty of the sexual landscape you've created. And you will have discovered a delightful outlet for your boundless creativity.

Finally, fantasy-sharing is so exciting it is nearly a sexual technological advance! By making your lover privy to what's going on in your mind, you allow him to see, touch, and *participate in* the steamiest scenes this side of interactive pornography! He doesn't feel alienated the way he would if he sensed you were thinking about something else while in the throes of sex. He is right there in the room, right there in bed, and right there in your mind. Knowing that he is an active player in the fantasies that make you weak with desire is tremendously stimulating for a man. And watching his mounting excitement will be tremendously stimulating for you! Your partner may even be inspired to "flesh out" the sensual scene with some erotic ideas of his own, thus setting off a tandem fantasy fest that can transport you both to the outermost limits of mutual pleasure.

Sex Talk Isn't Cheap. There's no question about it: sharing the cache of erotic thoughts you have buried like an erotic treasure is a bold move—and one that most sexually satisfied women take in stride. Yet for those women who weren't socialized to verbalize their desires, who aren't comfortable with sex as a bare-all proposition, this next logical step along the route to total sexual liberation can seem like a leap into the unknown.

When I met Jennie, she was thirty-one years old and the primary caregiver for her two pre-school-age children. Jennie revealed that the honeymoon had ended for her and her husband, Barry, long before the birth of their children. But if their marriage lacked sexual vigor before the blessed events, their intimacy—and Jennie's sexual satisfaction—hit rock bottom thereafter. Jennie began my program on a recommendation from a friend, and she was moving through the process with ease until she began thinking about fantasy-sharing. Then her inhibitions came to the fore.

"Wild Night was one thing. It was a game of pretend," she explained to me. "I enjoyed the power of playing the rock star my husband pants after, but since having groupies wasn't at the top of my own fantasy list it was easy for me to play along. After all, it was a scenario that didn't reveal anything new about my personal desires. But talking my way through fantasies I've actually *had*—not to mention those fantasies I'm *still* having—that hits pretty close to home. Wouldn't it put Barry into shock to know that I was supplementing our real sex life with daydreams? What if the fantasies that turn me on are a turnoff for him? And how about my secret thoughts about other men? Wouldn't revealing those ideas destroy my fantasies—and my marriage?"

I wasn't surprised to learn that Jennie, like countless other women, had been brought up in a household where women weren't supposed to have fantasies, much less reveal them. As Jennie described it, the very mention of the word *sex* was shocking to her mother. Years later, she was projecting that same negative reaction onto her husband, assuming—but not knowing—that he would think her cheap, uncontrollable, or even unfaithful if she shared her erotic imaginings with him.

But as I explained to Jennie, a woman's fantasies are an invaluable map to the sensual scenarios that rouse her mind and arouse her body. Without that map, a man could literally search forever—and never find the right combination of sexual touches that will bring his partner pleasure.

But what if that map leads your lover into a part of Wonderland that makes him wonder about *you?* What about those sexual fantasies that venture into the realm of the dark or secret or taboo—the forbidden zone of sexual thinking? Should you be afraid of those fantasies? The answer is no. Nothing can hurt you in Wonderland. Can you share them with a partner not knowing if he will find them upsetting? The answer is yes—with qualifications.

How Weird Is Weird? For some people, the idea of making love with their socks on is a walk on the wild side! For others, fantasies about group sex, lesbian sex, sadomasochistic encounters, or sex with the entire legislative branch of the United States government are old hat.

Do most people have sexual dreams that break the rules of sexual decorum? Most people not only have them, they enjoy them! Is there any reason to be frightened of such fantasies? Absolutely not. Wonderland is a realm of thought, an idea grounded in the principle of total sexual expression. Since nothing really happens in

Wonderland, there is simply no need for rules of sexual decorum. And since you are the architect of your own Wonderland, you should find nothing there that will frighten or intimidate you in any way.

True enough, even a sexual fantasy that doesn't seem weird in the having may seem incredibly weird in the telling. To bring your erotic secrets into the bedroom, you must first take them out of your head, and the sensual scenarios that seem perfectly acceptable in Wonderland may seem strange or even perverted in the context of your real life. Of course, having a sexual fantasy doesn't make you weird any more than having a feeling makes you weird. And since the same range of feelings is shared by all human beings, you don't have to look hard to see that common sexual themes underlie even the most outrageous fantasies. (Many women have discovered that mental images they considered offbeat were the same secret desires harbored by their husbands!)

Still, our erotic dreams *are* unique to us. In fact, they are a lot like our nocturnal dreams: personal, revelatory, creatively scripted, and wildly embellished by our imaginations. Certainly there is no right or wrong when it comes to the fantasies we enjoy during sleep. So why should we label those mental images that bring us sexual pleasure? Every woman's sexual fantasies are right for her. Your fantasies are right for you because they reflect what you have experienced and felt over your lifetime.

So which sexual fantasies are the "right" ones to share with your partner? The answer is, *any fantasy you have* can be shared out loud with your partner during sex—as long as it is revealed in a way that does not threaten or upset him.

Two's Company . . . Three's a Fantasy. Most men—particularly the lucky partners of the sexually satisfied women who have passed through this program—consider fantasy-sharing a welcome addition to their sexual repertoire. And why not? Fantasy-sharing is a safe way to explore sexual desires without actually *acting* on sexual desires—and nothing could be less threatening than that. Others feel that fantasy-sharing is a lively and liberating solution to every marital problem from prolonged monogamy to sexual monotony. Through the magic of fantasy, they can experience coital feats and erotic treats they could never aspire to in real life, including the impractical (making love on the receptionist's desk at work), the unfeasible (intercourse in a tree), the physically unsafe (making love in a speeding convertible), the illegal (making love in a public place), and even the outright impossible (making love in zero gravity in a crater of the moon). Sharing the fantasies of the women they love takes these men to places they otherwise could not go and sets their imagination soaring. It is the only sexual technique that is not limited to time, space or reality.

For a small percentage of men, however, certain fantasies are out of bounds, particularly those that call the masculine ego into question. To these men, just knowing that you fantasize at all can be perceived as a threat. Knowing that you fantasize about other men is akin to adultery.

If you are involved with a man like that, it may help you to know that you cannot be unfaithful to your partner by having a fantasy—*any* fantasy. Provocative mental images are thoughts, not deeds, and while your lover may have something to say about the things you do, no one has a license on your ideas, images, fantasies, or anything else that goes on in your mind.

You should also know that there is a sharp distinction between the two kinds of men who appear in your fantasies. Accessible men are the physically attainable males you know. Inaccessible men are the movie stars or faceless, idealized strangers who appear in your erotic dreams to do *your* sexual bidding.

Since only real men pose real threats, feel free to share your fantasies about inaccessible men with your partner—provided he can handle them. If he becomes upset or angry, explain that you are neither cheating on him nor comparing him to a fantastic ideal. Or smooth things over with the Great Turn-off Turnaround explained on page 124. Generally I find that these envy issues are talked about once or twice, then forgotten.

As for the accessible man—the coworker, friend, or other reachable male who plays a part in your life as well as in your sexual imaginings—weigh your decision to reveal his identity with care. If the fantasy is a fleeting, one-time fancy or a passing curiosity and you feel your lover would be comfortable with it, I would say go ahead and share it. You may find that talking the fantasy through once or twice will put your curiosity to rest.

If, on the other hand, you have a recurring fantasy about an accessible man, particularly one that prevents you from enjoying sex with your partner, you *must* confront the fantasy with your partner. It will not go away—and it *can* contain the seeds of infidelity.

Approach the subject with sensitivity, and try to enlist your lover's help by conveying to him a sense of common purpose. Say something like, "Honey, I keep having this fantasy about ———, and it is getting in

the way of enjoying sex with you. I don't really want to
think about this, and I certainly don't want to act on it,
but I think we both need to understand it. Will you
help me get to the bottom of this, so that nothing gets
in the way of our happiness?" This sort of recurring fantasy expresses an unfulfilled need in you. It is critical
that you find out what that need is and fulfill it within
your relationship in order to avert temptation—or the
deterioration of your sexual partnership.

By the way, it will be helpful if you discuss these feelings with your partner in a nonsexual setting. Men are
most vulnerable during sex, and this kind of "heavy"
revelation could easily turn the lovemaking experience
into a negative one. Your partner could lose his erection, for example, which would be embarrassing for him
and awkward for you. Only you can decide when the
time is right to tell him. Use your intuition but don't
use the bedroom. That special meeting ground is
strictly reserved for the kind of fantasies you can share
and enjoy with confidence, such as the provocative images and sizzling scenarios you'll be gathering momentarily in Wonderland.

Preliminary Step 1: A Visit to Wonderland

You've heard of information gathering? Well, this is
titillation gathering!

The goal of this exercise is to help you enter your
own fantasy world—the Wonderland in your mind—so
you will have some fantasies on hand when you begin
the fantasy-sharing process. Creativity inspires creativity. As you become more comfortable with fantasy-
sharing, you will undoubtedly come up with plenty of
new fantasies on your own; but initially you will want

to have some favorite fantasies at the ready so you can concentrate on learning the fantasy-sharing technique.

This exercise is designed to lead you to the most spectacular landmarks in Wonderland: your most arousing sexual fantasies. It will be a true pleasure trip. You may recall that in chapter 2 I asked you to list the sexual fantasies that most readily came to mind for you. You may want to go back and review that list now as preparation for this excursion. If you did not perform the exercise, consider going back and doing it now—or make the list immediately after this trip to Wonderland. There are more than enough fantastic fantasies within this exercise to fire your imagination.

Relax in bed or settle into a comfortable chair, clothes on or off, as you desire. Now close your eyes and focus on one of your favorite fantasies—or explore one of the sexual scenarios below. Imagine . . .

- Being aroused by a sexual act you've never tried before, such as oral sex, anal sex, mutual masturbation, or "breast intercourse." Conjure up a stimulating setting for your "first time," and embellish the scenario as you wish.

- Enjoying a new and intriguing position, such as intercourse while seated, while standing or in the "female superior" or "woman on top" position, or simultaneous oral sex in the "sixty-nine" position.

- Stimulating your partner in a new way, perhaps rubbing your breasts all over his body, licking his toes, or massaging his penis from behind in the shower.

- Making love in a fabulously novel location: in a different room of your home, in a log cabin in the mountains; or on a private, secluded beach with the water lapping gently at your body.

- Using sex toys to bring a playful spirit to the bedroom. How would it feel to use a vibrator or massager on yourself during intercourse? Which erogenous zones would come alive with the touch of a feather? What would it be like to watch yourself in flagrante delicto in a ceiling mirror or to videotape your activities for posterity?

- Exploring how "naughty" you can really be. How would it feel if your partner overpowered you and tied you lightly to the bed? Would it stimulate you if you were to get a few playful "love taps" on your bottom? What would it be like to have your partner order you around, "make" you do things to him sexually, make you his "love slave"? Would it be more stimulating if you were the one in control? (Remember: these are fantasies—and fantasies do not have to be acted out.)

- Having two, three, or more men make love to you at the same time. Concentrate on the attention you would receive.

- Being taken by surprise when you are least expecting it—by your partner or by the stranger of your dreams.

- Meeting your partner (or a stranger) and, without ever exchanging a word, ripping off each other's clothes and engaging in raw, urgent, passionate, animalistic sex.

Once you have settled on a fantasy—your own or one of the above—focus your attention on a single compelling aspect of the scenario, such as an isolated image, an object (perhaps a piece of clothing), a sound (panting), a smell (your lover's scent), a physical sensation, a color, a texture, a movement, a gesture, or the sexual act itself.

Now shift your concentration to one or more of the broader issues in the fantasy, such as the mood, the setting, the lighting, the atmosphere, or the environment. (If the fantasy fits, you might, for example, focus on the fact that you and your partner are on horseback in the moonlight with the wind blowing through your hair.) Concentrate on the images you see, but go with the flow when your imagination takes off in different directions. If, for instance, smaller details and points of focus broaden into a full-fledged plot, allow the drama to unfold. Let the fantasy flesh itself out until it becomes a self-directed story and an ever-changing scenario.

Don't busy your mind consciously inventing fiction; just let your mind run away with your feelings. And don't force the plot toward any particular conclusion; simply allow your imagination to soar, secure in the knowledge that your mind will find its own happy ending. If you begin to have sensual or sexual feelings at any time during the fantasy, accept them and allow them to overtake you. Let yourself sink into your own pleasure and indulge it as you see fit.

Finally, let the fantasy run its course. Let your mind and feelings exhaust themselves until there is nothing left to the fantasy—and just the merest consciousness left of you. Then, if you have any energy left, focus on another sensual scene from your repertoire and perform the procedure again. If not, take a deep breath, open your eyes, and allow your body and mind to return to reality.

You may repeat this exercise many times, exploring as many different areas of Wonderland as you like, until you feel ready to begin sharing your experiences with your partner. One warning, though: be careful not to use this exercise as an "escape" or as an excuse to retreat into masturbatory lovemaking—intercourse in which you keep your thoughts to yourself for private pleasure. Your goal is to gather intriguing images that *two* can share. Use the material for its purpose: to rev up your sex life *with* your partner. It will make every erotic encounter twice as satisfying for you.

Preliminary Step 2: Preparing Your Partner for Wonderland

If you have worked through the chapters of this book, your partner has learned from experience that fulfilling your sexual wants doesn't leave him wanting for anything! Once you let on that you are planning to take your sexuality into a new dimension, he'll be raring to go along for the ride.

Since tantalizing your man with your fantasies is a form of PowerTeasing in itself, preparing your lover for Wonderland will be a pleasure for both of you. One night *after* you have made love, drop the subject in his lap by saying simply, "Honey, next time we make love I'd like to tell you about some of my fantasies." Then wait. Your lover will undoubtedly be intrigued enough to ask what kind of fantasies you have in mind. When he does, serve up a little taste of your most delicious imaginings. You'll make him hungry for more, or you'll get him so aroused that he'll demand seconds, right then and there.

If your man is partial to erotic ambush, you can also broach the subject during the day, at a time when he least expects it. Approach him in the middle of a task, give him a bit of a physical tweak, then whisper in his ear, "I'm going to tell you about some of my fantasies tonight. And you're going to love it!" Then walk away as if nothing had happened. The longtime lover of a vintage-car collector got the ball rolling by lying back on a mechanic's dolly, rolling under the car her husband was overhauling, and delivering her provocative message while her husband was up to his elbows in grease! He cleaned up in a hurry—and she cleaned out some of the fantasies that had been collecting dust in her Wonderland.

This preliminary step is not critical, so if you feel uncomfortable about warning your man about your plans, or if you would simply prefer to get right to it, just read on. Springing the activity on him during a lovemaking encounter puts the element of surprise on your side—and that can be extremely exciting in itself.

Preliminary Step 3: Choosing the Setting

Fantasy-sharing is a surefire way to turn up the heat on your love affair. But sexual temperature is like the weather. Some like it hot. They want their sex lives to sizzle, so they stay as close as possible to the sources of erotic heat. Others must ease into a new situation and prefer to maintain their cool until they do.

Fantasy-sharing is always hot, but it is possible to warm up to it slowly. It depends on the setting you choose to introduce it. The three scenarios below range in intensity from a comfortable telephone tease to an all-out, face-to-face, fantasy blitz. Since fantasies flow most freely when you're relaxed, it is best to select a medium for your message that is well within your personal comfort zone. Acclimatize yourself by reading through the following scenarios. Then select the one that seems just hot enough for you to handle.

On the Telephone. If you are shy about revealing your most intimate thoughts and want to put a comfortable distance between you and your lover, talking out your fantasies over the phone may be the way to break the sexual sound barrier. It is also a terrific method for safely testing your partner's reaction to what you've got to say.

If you have two telephone lines at home, you can phone your partner from one room (preferably a room with a bed!) while he listens in another. Since your partner will only be with you in spirit, you can stimulate yourself—manually or with a vibrator—as you speak to achieve the simultaneous emotional and physical benefit of this technique.

If you have one phone line at home, you can still make the connection by using a phone with a built-in "intercom" button. Or ask the phone company to make your existing phone intercom-capable for a month or two. This feature allows you to speak, without static, on two different extensions of the same line. You can beep your partner from one phone and have him pick up another, as if you were making an outside call. When you call your partner, do as described above: lie in bed, undressed, and stimulate yourself while you reveal your fantasies to him.

If neither of the above methods is workable, simply

have your partner call you from another location, per-haps when he can steal a few peaceful moments from work. Of course, this option doesn't allow for any im-mediate fireworks. Still, it is a great tease—and should ensure an interesting evening to come.

During Stimulation. Adding a new technique to your sexual repertoire can add pressure to lovemaking. This option stops short of actual intercourse so you and your partner can explore the unique pleasures of fantasy-sharing without having to deal with perform-ance anxiety. Arrange a time—during regular love-making or at a relaxed hour—when you and your partner are in the mood for a "meeting of the minds." When you are ready, ask your partner to stimulate you—manually or orally—while you describe the erotic images that flow through your mind.

During Lovemaking. The option of choice for sexual spitfires (and anyone aspiring to spitfiredom!), this will bring you face-to-face with your partner as well as with your fantasies. This option can take regular lovemaking to dizzying heights—with dazzling results.

Of course, no matter which scenario you choose, fantasy-sharing inspires anything but an ordinary sexual encounter. Driven by your most urgent desires, shaped by your boundless creativity, fantasy-sharing allows each sexual experience to invent and reinvent itself, in tandem with your emerging thoughts. The ultimate body/mind connection, it is a direct route to total re-lease, limited only by your physical stamina.

Fantasy-sharing requires only three steps: imagine (focus on your fantasies); talk (reveal your thoughts);

and feel (connect physically with the scenario unfolding in your mind). However, to broaden your understanding of this technique and to help you bring your partner more fully into your Wonderland, I have included two additional steps. It won't be long before the entire process becomes second nature to you.

THE FANTASY-SHARING TECHNIQUE

Step 1: Imagine

Whether you're on the phone with your partner or under his touch, close your eyes and focus on one of the fantasies you imagined in Preliminary Step 1, one you would like to share verbally with your partner.

As you did in the preliminary exercise, focus on a single aspect of the fantasy, such as a sexual act, a specific image, or a sensation. When you can "feel" the effect of the image you've chosen, broaden your focus. Concentrate on the mood, setting, location, or atmosphere. Allow the imagery to develop a bit, until it is vivid and arousing.

Step 2: Talk

When you feel ready, begin to describe the scene as it is developing in your mind. Center your attention on parts of the sexual image that are especially stimulating for you—and don't be embarrassed to communicate your passion to your partner. Your arousal will only entice him further into the Wonderland you are describing.

A fantasy can be as straightforward as a single act of

love or as complex and dramatic as an Italian opera. Be true to what you see in your mind's eye. If you're having trouble breaking the ice, begin with a simple one- or two-sentence statement, such as:

- I see myself rubbing my breasts all over your body.

- I want to hold you down on the bed so you can't escape, then climb on top of you and put you inside me.

- You're a construction worker who has just gotten home from work. You want me so badly that you throw your hard hat aside and take me on the living room carpet.

- I'm imagining what it feels like to have four hands running over my body at once.

- We're making love in a mirrored room. I'm watching in a large mirror that's suspended over the bed. I'm excited by the way we look making love.

- You're a complete stranger to me. Though we've just met in a nightclub, I want to take you to the ladies room and do you up right.

- I'd love to have you take me by surprise one night, when I'm not expecting it.

- I see us up in the mountains, making love in a log cabin during a rainstorm, with the rain pitter-pattering against the window.

Step 3: Feel

As you begin to talk about what you see, get in touch with your sexual feelings. Put your consciousness on hold and let the words spill out while you physically connect with what you hear yourself saying. In other words, let your talk turn you on. Free association—that is, the uncensored release of images and emotions—and physical stimulation are totally separate phenomena. Your goal now is to bring the two together so that the vivid scenarios that stimulate your mind can awaken the pleasure centers of your body.

Let your words "caress" you the way your partner's hand might lovingly caress you. Imagine that the ideas you're talking about have taken shape and are working their magic on your erogenous zones.

When you hear yourself describing an exciting scene or image and it seems as though the words are coming not from you but from an impartial observer, you have hit the mark. Now expand on the fantasy. Open it up a little bit. Move from one image to another, or one act to another, always allowing yourself time to connect your words with your feelings. Before you know it, your imagination will begin working automatically. Graphic scenes and erotic images will pop, full-blown, into your mind. Reveal them as they appear, permitting yourself (and your partner) the blissful indulgence of sinking deeper and deeper under the spellbinding power of your words.

Step 4: Encourage Your Partner's Participation

Fantasy-sharing generates a great deal of sexual energy. Indeed, your partner may be so invigorated by this experience that he already has become part of your Wonderland, urging you on to greater heights of passion or adding to the fantasy himself.

If he is obviously excited but keeping his thoughts to himself, he may be waiting for an invitation into what he regards as your private world. That invitation is easy to send. Simply spin your tale as vividly as possible, then—when you know your lover is hanging on your every word—murmur playfully, "Do you want to hear more?"

Whether he is mesmerized by this new facet of lovemaking or drawn on by the urgency of his own erection, he will certainly urge you on. If necessary, you can use the invitation like a tease, pausing at critical points in the plot until he demands that you tell him more: "And then what?" "Go on!" "I like that!" "That's it!" "Yes! Yes!"

Ideally, you want to get him to participate in *your* fantasy. If he begins to add ideas of his own or to use the opportunity to live out one of his own fantasies, you have several options. If his ideas pique your interest, follow his path to see where it goes. (Getting a glimpse of someone else's Wonderland is enough to bring out the happy voyeur in any of us!) If you prefer, maintain control and stay the course of your own fantasy, but incorporate some of the ideas that meet his needs. That scenario would go something like this:

You: I want to hold you down on the bed and tease your penis between my thighs.

He: Can you tie me to the bedposts?

You: Yes, but only *after* you've done what I want you to.

Voila! You've promised to fulfill his erotic dream and given him incentive to please you without taking anything away from *your* fantasy.

If your partner gets turned off by anything you see in Wonderland or becomes upset or offended, you needn't let it spoil the mood. The Great Turn-off Turnaround is a technique that enables you to explore a fantasy's wildest possibilities without offending your lover's sensibilities. To do it, break your vision into smaller parts. If, for example, you have a fantasy of making it with three men at the same time and that idea is not making it with your lover, effect a compromise that moves you step by step toward the fulfillment of your erotic dream. You might begin by saying something like: "I'm imagining what it would be like to have you massage my breasts and play with my clitoris at the same time. Oooh, does that feel good!"

Later in the fantasy, or during another fantasy-sharing session, take the idea further: "It drives me crazy to think about you stimulating more than one part of my body. It gives me the sensation of four hands caressing me at once. It feels so good!"

Then, when he seems ready, you can follow it up with a line like this one: "Now I'm imagining what it would be like if someone else were joining you while you made love to me. Mmmm . . . think about the possibilities."

Keep going until you have two, three, or a boatload of partners—whatever it takes to fulfill the fantasy.

Step 5: Open the Floodgates

Opening yourself to fantasy-sharing is like opening Pandora's box. Once you've blown the lid off your erotic dreams and given your lover a tantalizing peek inside, you have no choice but to go with the flow! Every emotion, thought, and erotic idea you've ever repressed is on its way out in a tremendous rush to fulfillment. Begin with the current fantasy. Give yourself up to it without judgment. Let it wash over you like a powerful, invigorating waterfall then carry you away in a current of pleasure.

Say exactly what's on your mind. Don't censor yourself, don't hold yourself back—and don't be embarrassed to say the things you would not say in polite company. Remember, Wonderland is a strange and wonderful place. You may be surprised by the curious nooks and crannies of your mind, but the resulting release is truly a wonder.

If your fantasies take an unexpected detour, or if they change course entirely, follow them to their ultimate destination. Go where they want to take you. Let them be your guide. What begins as a seemingly mild pleasure trip can lead you to something much more exciting. You may discover a recurring theme that links your fantasies or strengthens the bond between you and your partner. You may even discover a complex sexual story that you would like to live out through play-acting—a technique I describe fully in the next chapter.

Where Do You Go from Here? Anywhere and everywhere your erotic dreams lead you! Fantasies don't exhaust themselves (like lovers do!). They beget even richer fantasies. If your first taste of adventure has whetted your appetite for unexplored territory, you may decide to search the outermost reaches of Wonderland for the most inventive new fantasies you can find. You may choose an undeveloped aspect of today's fantasy to build on. Or, for a lip-smacking taste of your own medicine, you may suggest to your partner that he talk out one of *his* fantasies.

Wherever your fantasies lead you, no matter which route to your ultimate satisfaction you choose, you will find that, with time, your fantasies will build on each other. Before long, you will begin to get a panoramic view of your Wonderland, not as a limited state of mind, but as an ever-expanding vista filled with enticing twists, gratifying turns, and endlessly intriguing detours. To any woman searching for satisfaction, it is beautiful terrain indeed.

QUESTIONS AND ANSWERS ABOUT FANTASY-SHARING

Fantasy-sharing is a daring—and often misunderstood—technique. What follows are several of the most common questions I am asked about the activity. These questions address the specific fears revealed to me by private clients, as well as by women who have attended my seminars. The solutions I offered put those fears to rest.

What if my partner becomes upset by one of my fantasies, or offended, or turned off?

If your partner finds one of your fantasies upsetting, or offensive, or a turnoff, that doesn't mean you can't achieve fulfillment of the fantasy. Fantasies don't have to be either/or propositions. In other words, if he has a problem with the fantasy, you don't have to say to yourself, "Oh, well, I guess that's the end of the line for that fantasy—I'll never be able to talk it out with him." That's just not true. Fantasies can be modified, altered, and reshaped. You can modify a fantasy in a way that makes it acceptable to your partner and still allows you to find fulfillment.

No matter what the basis of your partner's objection, no matter how inflexible he seems, I suggest that you break your fantasy into palatable pieces, and feed him one morsel at a time, as described in the Great Turn-off Turnaround (page 124).

Suppose your fondest fantasy centers on an activity your partner is reluctant to perform—oral sex, for example. You can ease into your desires (and get him in the vicinity of your Wonderland) by suggesting an innocuous compromise such as: "It would be so nice if you would rub my legs." If he seems willing to carry along the idea, you can begin to narrow the target area in your collective vision. You could direct him mentally by saying, "It would be so nice if you would kiss my legs." Or, "It would feel really good if you would kiss and lick my stomach and belly button." Then, "It would turn me on if you would kiss me in the little hollow where my legs join my hips."

Slowly but surely, step by step, make your way closer and closer to your goal in your mind and his. If he balks, emphasize to him that this is only a fantasy and fantasies do not have be acted out (although you probably will want him to explore this sexual option eventually). If he allows his thoughts to roam near the spot, great. He may be just near enough for you to fulfill the fantasy.

Fantasies are not a one-way street. You may have to give up a little ground in consideration of your partner's sexual preferences, but you don't have to give up on your fantasy. Take it step by step, be creative, and pretty soon you'll have your partner "eating out of your hand."

What if my partner thinks I'm strange, or weird, because of one of my fantasies?

To label someone's fantasy as strange or weird is to judge that person unfairly. If your partner uses these terms with you, or dismisses your normal fantasies in any way, he is being unfair to you and your sexuality. No one has the right to judge another person's thoughts or feelings unless they involve the potential for physical harm or emotional abuse.

Remember: Wonderland is a strange and unusual place. It does not follow the social mores of Anytown, USA. It is a state of mind and, as such, is governed only by your feelings. (And feelings are *always* acceptable, again unless they point to physical harm or emotional abuse.)

Here's a metaphor that may help you to get the picture. A television turns electronic frequencies into visual images. Your mind converts emotions into sexual images. Depending on the make and history of your "set" and the range and power of your emotions, you may tune in on some rather peculiar images—including some that don't do much for your lover's horizontal hold. Nevertheless, that does not mean there's anything "wrong" with your mindset—or with you.

If your partner is oppressively judgmental about your erotic visions, he is revealing an uptight attitude about *his* sexuality. And if he describes your fantasies (or you) as kinky or perverted, he is expressing a selfish disregard for *your* sexuality. If he were willing to look inside himself and report honestly on the status of his own Wonderland, he would reveal sexual fantasies that are every bit as unusual as yours. Admit it or not, *everyone* has strange fantasies on occasion. They merely reflect the range of intense emotions human beings can feel.

You may be afraid your partner will reject you, or even leave you, because of your fantasies. For the most part this is an irrational fear, but I can't say that it never happens. If it does come down to a choice, you must evaluate which is more important: keeping your partner or becoming free within yourself. It's sort of like comparing hands in a game of poker. Self-fulfillment and inner satisfaction are the "royal flush" of life. Keeping a partner just for the sake of keeping him, even though you must deny a part of yourself, is at best the equivalent of a "full house." Both hands have their merits, but only one hand wins.

If your partner is truly offended by one of your fantasies, you might try the Great Turn-off Turnaround described earlier. But if the fantasy expresses a significant part of your mental life, how can you deny it? You need not threaten your partner, but you must let him know gently and compassionately that you feel the need to express yourself—without censure—so that nothing gets in the way of your sexual enjoyment with him. Make your sexual liberation a joint project. Explain that you want him to *help* you uncover your blocks so that you can be fully present with him during sex. This persuasive you-and-me-against-the-world approach can not only make him more willing to look at the fantasy in question, it may even encourage him to reconsider his own ideas about what is strange and what is not.

What if I become obsessed with a fantasy and keep thinking about it over and over again?

If a fantasy occupies your mind repeatedly *before* you express it to your partner, the best thing to do is to fantasy-share it with him a few times in bed. Nothing gathers strength over time like a secret. It may take a number of fantasy-sharing sessions before you are able get your "secret" out of your system.

If the fantasy persists, if it continues to gather strength, and—most important—if it is troubling to you, then it may be the manifestation of an underlying emotional issue or a feeling that has been left unre-solved.

I suggest that you continue to share the fantasy with your partner over additional lovemaking sessions, con-centrating on the feelings you experience as you do. The deeper reason for the fantasy may suddenly spring into your conscious mind—even pop out of your mouth during free association. If it does, don't fight it—and don't fear it. Experience it, and let it express what it wants to express. Once you have brought the feeling to light, the fantasy may simply disappear.

If, however, the specter continues to nag you, I sug-gest you seek counseling to help you trace the problem back to its root. Such a fantasy indicates an *unfulfilled need*. A warm, comfortable, supportive counseling envi-ronment will help you uncover, understand, and resolve that need. The fantasy will either loosen its grip on you and vanish altogether or be transformed into a pleasur-able scenario—one that is subject to your desires. Such fantasies offer a tremendous opportunity for self-discovery, so rather than run from them, embrace them.

They are a rare opportunity to find out who you really are inside.

I'm afraid that if I try fantasy-sharing I'll lose control and wind up doing strange things sexually. Can such a thing happen?

First let's look at the phrase *lose control*. What does it mean? If you are afraid of losing control, you are afraid of being overcome by passion. If you have ever experienced orgasm (and a recent study indicates that 90 percent of women have experienced an orgasm by age thirty-five), then you have certainly experienced the total loss of control. *Nothing you experience as a result of fantasy-sharing will cause any more of a "loss of control" than you experience in orgasm.*

It is also likely that your fear of losing control bisects all of the aspects of your life—not just your sexuality. Ask yourself: do you express yourself openly or do you keep everything inside? Can you cry in public? Can you laugh? Can you express anger when you feel it? If the answer to most of these questions is no, you are a person who keeps an extremely tight grip on her emotions. What is strange for you may be the norm for a great many people.

As for the possibility that you might "do strange things sexually," so what if you do? Look at it this way: by acting on your desires, you may give yourself the opportunity to overcome an inhibition. And at the very least, you will learn what you like and don't like. Perhaps your fear is that you will do something that, afterwards, you'll be ashamed of or put off by—like lick your partner from head to toe. Yet once you do it, only then will you know if it is something you like. And keep in mind that fantasies—and fears—are always stronger in our minds until we do something about them. After you do what it is you're afraid of, you may find that there was nothing to *be* afraid of.

But nobody can make you do anything you don't want to do. Nor does anyone want to. And you always have the option to keep fantasies as fantasies, without ever acting on them. After all, this is fantasy-sharing. Talking through what you see in your mind's eye is just that: talking. When you move into the realm of physical action, you are entering the arena of play-acting. I hope that by reading the chapter on play-acting you will gain some sense of comfort—and liberation—about the pleasures of acting out sexually. But play-acting is always a choice, and you can gain as much fulfillment from sharing fantasies as from acting on them.

Remember: Wonderland is an unusual place, and the ideas that come from Wonderland may strike you as very odd. In bed, you may find yourself compelled to do any number of things you have never done before. It is your choice to do them or not, as you see fit. And if your fear is that you will enjoy doing something you cannot admit wanting to do, remember that fears are inhibitions, and inhibitions—to borrow a line from the movie *Klute*—"are great because they are so much fun to overcome."

Personally, I prefer the converse of this question. It would go something like this: "If I try fantasy-sharing, will I let myself go sexually and wind up doing everything I've ever wanted to do in bed?" If you let go of your fears you will. And what could be better than that?

I have a nagging fear that if I try fantasy-sharing I might literally go out of my mind. Is this at all possible?

I hope you do go out of your mind—out of your mind with pleasure!

But the fear of losing one's mind is a restatement of the fear of losing control, only in the extreme. It bears repeating, then, that the amount of control you will lose during fantasy-sharing is commensurate with the "meltdown" you experience during an orgasm. I don't have to tell you that no one ever went crazy because of an orgasm. There is no true-confession book I know of entitled *The Orgasm That Drove Me Insane*.

If you are truly concerned about the effect of your fantasies on your mental status, it is likely there is a feeling you are afraid to confront, and that feeling is entering your consciousness through your erotic imagination. In that case, you may be burying your fantasies to keep your feelings out of sight. Or you may be fearful that letting go during sex will set the feeling loose, enable it to overwhelm you, and cause you to lose control of your faculties.

The beauty of feelings is that by expressing them you experience relief. If you find that you are afraid of a particular sexual fantasy, or you sense that you fear having to face a feeling that you've been hiding, try to muster up the courage to confront the feeling by sharing the fantasy with your partner. If you can get past your fear and release your bottled-up emotion, your relief will be instantaneous.

If you cannot confront the fantasy or the feeling, or if you feel too intimidated to try fantasy-sharing, then I recommend that you consider seeking professional counseling to help you face your fear. You owe it to yourself to get the most out of your sex life, and you deserve to enjoy the rare pleasures that fantasy-sharing can bring.

Once I try fantasy-sharing, will I ever be able to have "regular" sex again, or will I only be able to get stimulated by sharing my fantasies?

Fantasy-sharing is not addictive in the negative sense, but it *is* addictive in the positive sense: once you try it, you will probably want to experience again and again the emotional and physical high it brings you.

It may reassure you to know that no law of the mind or body says that once you open the floodgates of fantasies, the only way you will be able to get physical stimulation is by continuing to channel your fantasies outward. In fact, once you become comfortable with fantasy-sharing, once you can focus less on the technique and more on the fantasies themselves, you will find that it is just another option in your sexual repertoire—an option you can turn to or turn off at will.

Frankly, I'm more concerned with your definition of "regular" sex than I am with the possibility of "addiction." What sort of sex is regular to you? Sex in the missionary position? Sex without talking, breathing, or moaning? The kind of sex that the pitchfork-holding farmer and his grim-lipped wife in the Grant Wood painting, *American Gothic*, would probably have—if they dared to indulge? If that's the kind of socially acceptable sex you had in mind, it'd be a quantum leap backward—straight into the boudoir of the perennially bored.

But if by regular sex you mean adventurous sex without sharing fantasies, then the answer is yes: you can certainly get gratifying physical stimulation without the use of fantasies. Just bear in mind that you can heighten your enjoyment, add variety to your sexual repertoire, and become a more satisfied woman, all by taking a vacation from "regular" sex and visiting the Fantasy Island of your mind!

I'm afraid of what my family, friends, colleagues, and neighbors would think if they ever found out what kind of sexual fantasies I have. Is this a reasonable fear?

This open book may be having a transformational effect on your sex life, but that doesn't mean your sex life is an open book. Are your relatives, colleagues, and friends so astute that they can actually read into your deepest thoughts and fantasies? If they could, they would be privy to your private thoughts about them. Would they still be your friends?

Is it possible that in sharing your fantasies with a partner, these erotic imaginings are somehow broadcast to the world at large? Only if your walls are exceptionally thin—and your neighbors are exceptionally nosy!

Is your partner likely to announce to all and sundry that your sexual fantasies are the *real* cause of global warming? Only if he's a low-down cad—with a lover who's about to become very popular!

The truth is, it is highly unlikely that anyone would find out about your fantasies—unless, of course, you tell them. If you would like to talk about your fantasies to someone other than your partner, I advise you to do so *only* if you feel that person can handle the discussion sensibly, can be receptive and tolerant of your fantasies, *and* can maintain strict confidentiality on this very private part of your life.

Of course, if you have no problem about sharing your fantasies with anyone and everyone, you are free to do so. But keep in mind that society still casts a dark eye on certain aspects of sexuality. The tabloids have made millions on the penchants of the rich and famous. Your secret proclivities can come back to haunt you, too—usually when you least expect it.

That said, what if someone *does* find out that you harbor a burning desire for sex on a hook-and-ladder truck? Take a lesson from an earlier answer and don't let anyone judge you for it. Walk tall and hold your wildly creative head high. Your Wonderland is the key to your sexual satisfaction. You need make no apologies for your now-obvious-to-everyone fulfillment.

And as for any person who dares look askance at you, here's a proverb that should give you some solace: Who is he who casts the first stone? A busybody with hidden fantasies of his own! In other words, if your nemesis were truly fulfilled, if he were able to satisfy his own sexual fantasies, he would have no need to cast aspersions in your direction.

In the pursuit of sexual satisfaction, you may exhaust your body, you may exhaust your partner, but you will never exhaust the natural resources of Wonderland. I know that fantasy-sharing is a bold break from long-term sexual passivity. Be confident in the knowledge that you are getting in touch with the unknown parts of yourself, that you are well on the way to finding sexual satisfaction. I also know that the greatest barrier to intimacy is fear. Be proud that you have been able to throw open the doors of your Wonderland, throw off the shackles of your inhibitions, and take all the sexual pleasure you deserve. Now only one step remains: taking your sexual pleasure to the ultimate limits! As you will see in the next chapter, that's as easy as play-acting.

8 〜

*The Pleasures of Play-acting:
Acting out Your Fantasies for
Maximum Sexual Excitement*

〜

You can call it role-playing. You can call it "dress up." You can call it a game of let's pretend or sexual make believe. But the one thing you will never call play-acting is dull. Raucous and ribald, play-acting is an exciting change of pace that will change your view of sex (and your role in it) forever. Campy and creative, lively and licentious, play-acting is also the most fun you can have wearing clothes, using props, experimenting with settings, teasing with sex toys—and bringing all your favorite fantasies to life.

Make no mistake about it: fantasy-sharing is a satisfying all-talk, some-action alternative to reality-based sex. But when you play-act, your fantasy *becomes* the reality. You are released from the bounds of the here and now. And you are given one of the greatest sexual gifts of all: an infinitely expanding role in the unfolding drama of your sexual destiny.

Since thespian sex isn't about talking but *doing,* I'm going to cut to the chase (a popular play-acting option) and get right to the preliminaries. Through these simple introductory steps, you will develop a deep understanding of what play-acting—in all its forms—really is. You'll also learn how acting out can bring out the best side of any sexual encounter and set the stage for maximum sexual satisfaction.

Preliminary Step 1: Choose Your Role

There are no small roles in sexual role-playing, but two distinctly different kinds of roles are available to the sexual Thespian: the Dramatic Blockbuster and the Walk-on (the wild side).

As stars of the Dramatic Blockbuster, you and your partner play the parts of specific characters and bring your fantasies to life in a full-scale erotic production for two. If you have followed the "script" of my program so far, such a drama should not be a "cold read" for you. You've encountered these sorts of scenarios or vignettes before, most notably during Wild Night. Of course, the Dramatic Blockbuster is brought to you courtesy of the creative inhabitants of Wonderland, and since there are no rules in Wonderland, your blockbuster is not limited to any theme, plot, or even sexual subtext. You and your partner can share top billing in any scenario that captures your imagination: naïve schoolgirl and worldly teacher; Army officer and buck (naked) private; even bodice-ripping extravaganzas such as the seduction scene between Scarlett O'Hara and Rhett Butler.

If the Dramatic Blockbuster is the erotic version of a technicolor dream (and it is!), the Walk-on (the wild side) is the skin-to-skin equivalent of cinema verité. Walk-on roles aren't linked by any particular theme, nor do they feature any specific characters. But they do provide a fascinating framework for your desires—and a magical stage upon which you can act out any sexual acts, exotic techniques, naughty games, or sensual activities you've experienced only in your imagination—until now!

The Audition. Trying on the wide range of roles available to the sexual thespian is like trying on hats. Some will be too constricting; others will seem too flowery, too austere, or too "done." But sooner or later you will find one that is really "you."

Since fantasies breed fantasies, it may help to browse through the minidramas below to get a feel for the kind of part you might enjoy playing to the hilt. If a certain vignette intrigues you, jot it down. If the costumes associated with a certain role light your fire, add that minidrama to your wish list, too. (Many, many of the women in my seminars made their play-acting debuts in roles that "required" them to wear provocative clothing. Sanctioned by the role, they could give themselves permission to buy the garter belts and peek-a-boo undies they've always wanted—but would never allow themselves to buy.)

Of course, if any of these examples inspires you to develop an idea of your own, go for it! Play-acting is at its best when it's scripted in Wonderland.

"TEACHER'S PET"

Scenario   You play a teacher who'll do anything in her considerable power to make the learning process exciting. Your partner plays a student with a great deal of undeveloped potential. To show your special feelings for him, you ask him to stay after class so you can tutor him in math. (You're going to teach him how one plus one equals two.) And if he misbehaves? You hope he does! You'd love to teach him a lesson he'll never forget.

Costuming Pull your hair back, put on your specs, and go for the schoolmarm look. Or play the young, sexy teacher in a miniskirt and high-heeled boots.

"THE C.E.O."

Scenario You are the Chief Executive Officer of a large corporation, and your partner is your personal secretary. You ask your partner to follow you into your "office," close the door behind him, and seat yourself in a suitably important-looking chair. You bark, "It has come to my attention that *you*, Mr. _____, have no idea how to get ahead in this company. The question is: do you know how to *give head* (oral sex) in this company? . . ."

Costuming Dress up in your best business suit, if you have one; borrow a jacket and tie from your partner if you don't. Wear glasses for that professional look, and put your hair up.

"THE CURE FOR WHAT AILS YOU"

Scenario   You play a doctor and your partner plays a patient who needs your attention. He has an unexplained "swelling" and you offer to take care of it.

Costuming   Drape yourself in antiseptic white, buy an inexpensive "mask" (the kind they sell in hardware stores will do nicely) and hang a toy stethoscope around your neck. For a realistic change of pace, pull on a pair of rubber gloves before you begin the examination. The "drag" of the rubber will be a new sensation for him. (Or medicate him where it hurts with some scented massage oil.) As for your partner's garb, a sheet and a smile will do.

"A TOUCH OF CLASS"

Scenario   You are a demanding high-class call girl and your partner is a customer willing to pay a high price for your services. You've spent enough time meeting men's needs, and now you are ready to make some demands of your own. You do a leisurely strip—and tease your man until his interest is apparent. But wait—until money has changed hands, this is a no-go situation. Continue the tease until your partner actually lays a sizable bill in your hands.

Costuming   You are definitely not the kind of tart any man can pick up on the street. Dress to titillate, but show good taste. If you have to, put a sexy new dress on your charge account. You might make enough in one evening to pay it off in full!

"MARIAN THE LIBRARIAN"

Scenario   She may have been an English major, but boy can she speak in tongues! With her thick glasses and stuffy, highbrow demeanor, Marian seems like the stereotypical lonely intellectual. Still, there is something about her a lonely student (your partner) finds intriguing. He is very attracted to Marian. He even offers to flip her pages in the biology aisle. At first, Marian rejects his advances, playing the prude. But at a certain point, the flesh becomes willing. Marian takes off her glasses, lets down her hair, and becomes the hungry vixen, taking her pleasure atop a library table.

Costuming   Every woman has at least one fashion foible hanging in her closet that looks dowdier on her than it did on the rack, so this should be an easy vignette to dress for. Make sure, however, that your Marian isn't wearing white cotton briefs underneath it all. Nothing makes the frumpy-to-fiery transformation complete like eye-popping undies.

"YOU'RE IN THE ARMY NOW"

Scenario   You are an Army drill sergeant and your partner is a private in your platoon. You're going to give him strict discipline, make him march to your tune, and, ultimately, make a real man out of him.

Costuming   In ten minutes at your local Army–Navy surplus store, you can outfit yourself completely and inexpensively for this scenario—right down to the medals on your chest! (One creative woman I know even found herself a pair of camouflage boxer shorts to wear under her olive drabs. She had no trouble enlisting her husband's help when the time came to take them off!)

"MEN AT WORK"

Scenario   Many women have entertained the fantasy of making love to a rough, muscular construction worker after he has spent a long day at work. And why not? Hale and hearty construction workers are "built strong to last long"—and so is this scenario. Play around with it. Pretend your living room is a work site and have your man whistle at you as you walk past. Tell him off, strut up to him, pound playfully on his biceps, then make passionate love to each other. Or imagine that, during a casual stroll, you've gotten an eyeful of a man who is built like a brick house—and now you're trying to break down his resistance to you. Or you can pretend that your handyman comes home drenched with sweat from a hard day of work, picks you up caveman style, and carries you off to the bedroom.

Costuming   Whether your lover happens to be an accountant, a dermatologist or a pro bowler, it's a snap to dress him up like a man who knows how to turn a screw. All you need are blue jeans (faded to show he has worked in them), a T-shirt (no sleeves, please, so you can see and feel his muscles), a thick leather belt (after all, it has to be strong to hold up his tools!), and work shoes or boots. If you want, add a lunch pail for authenticity—and load it with some hardworking sex toys. To cap it all off, get him a hard hat. They're extremely inexpensive and available at home-improvement centers, lumber outlets, and hardware stores.

"AN AFFAIR WITH A STRANGER"

Scenario   Arrange to meet your partner at an elegant place—a night club, a posh hotel, a fancy restaurant—where you can pretend to meet and seduce each other as strangers. To take this scenario to the limit, reserve a room at a hotel—or in a unique location in your home—where you can get to know each other in the biblical sense.

Costuming   A cinch! Dress in outfits neither of you has seen before.

"PASSION ALLEY"

Scenario   This variation on "An Affair with a Stranger" takes place at home in total silence. Pretend you and your partner have not been properly introduced. In a room of your home, you meet, size each other up, and then, without exchanging a single word, "tear" each other's clothes off and engage in raw, urgent, passionate, animalistic sex until you're both satisfied.

Costuming   A wig, an outfit that seems out of character for you—anything that makes you seem like an improper stranger.

"ONE YOUNG AND RESTLESS LIFE TO LIVE"

Scenario   You and your partner take on the roles of two of the characters in your favorite TV show and act out all the highly charged scenes they can't show on the screen. Or try enacting a scene from a racy or romantic novel.

Costuming   Take inspiration from your characters' on-screen look—or from the cover of the book that has launched your flight of fancy.

Certainly you and your partner can and should change roles as you see fit to accommodate your needs and desires. Just be sure to adapt the clothing suggestions to the role you are playing. It's a fascinating truth that clothing has a tremendous power to create a mood and evoke a feeling—especially in the bedroom. To prove it to yourself, simply conjure up the memory of what it feels like to wear a low-cut, strapless evening dress . . . then a business suit . . . then a pair of flannel pajamas. If you are able to imagine vividly the sensation of these changes, you will undoubtedly feel your erotic potential rise—or decline—as you do.

Of course, play-acting doesn't have to be a dress ball—not if you prefer to play out your technical inventiveness. For you, I have included a selection of what I call Varieties: unique sexual activities you may have dreamed about but never tried. You may use them exactly as they are scripted or as points of departure for your creative physical explorations.

- New sexual acts: for example, anal intercourse; mutual or simultaneous masturbation; oral sex (if you have never tried it).

- New positions: for example, the upside down position for oral sex, in which your partner stands with his back to the wall and holds you upside down while you stimulate each other orally.

- New techniques: for example, using food during lovemaking. You might get creative with your vegetables or bring a little ranch-style dip to the bedroom to add tang to the evening.

- New locations: rent a camper or RV for some sexy fun on the road; rendezvous with your partner in a remote area where no one can see you.

- New gimmicks: sex toys, enticing clothing, massagers, oils, feather dusters, lingerie, mirrors, videotaping—anything that elevates sex beyond the ordinary.

- Kinky pleasures: Tie each other lightly to the bed with silk scarves, stockings, socks, ribbons—even condoms! Keep the bonds loose if you're concerned about feeling too helpless. Or if you've been especially "naughty," playfully tap each other on the bottom.

- Love slaves: "Force" your partner to do naughty things to you; or switch roles and be your partner's sexual captive for the evening. Plead for leniency by telling him, "Please don't _____," then fill in the blank with something you desperately *want* him to do. Or pretend you are helplessly under his power and ask querulously, "What are you going to do to me?"

- Sneak attack: Ask your partner to take you by surprise one night; or erotically ambush him when sex is the last thing on his mind.

Play-acting does have limitations, most notably time and space. There may be some sexual fantasies you simply cannot physically act out—but that doesn't mean you can't simulate the *sensation* of experiencing them. The women in my seminars have been extremely creative in finding exciting ways to evoke the feeling of a fantasy without actually bringing it to life. One ingenious woman who wanted to experience the feeling of twenty tongues running up and down her body at once got her "licks" by asking her partner to tape small pieces of moist sponge to his arms and elbows and run them up and down her body. When she closed her eyes, she was able to imagine they were real tongues—and her partner was able to satisfy her curiosity. The reality of that situation would have appeared odd to the objective observer (then again, what sexual act wouldn't appear odd to an objective observer?), but the point is strictly down-to-earth: the only real limitation to fantasy fulfillment is your own ingenuity—and the compliance of a willing partner. Which leads us directly to the next introductory step:

Preliminary Step 2: Reveal the Scenario to Your Co-star

Every good director knows that actors can't work "cold." This is your chance to warm your partner up by telling him, in detail, all about the sexy scenario you have in your head—and your plans to bring it to life in bed.

Of course, you don't have to give him a laundry list of all your fantasies. Such previews can steal a blockbuster's thunder. Nor should you go into great depth about the plot. That might "exhaust" the fantasy. The key is to tell your partner just enough for him to play his role the way you want—and to intrigue him into helping you live out your dreams.

If you've worked through the various phases of the Sexual Satisfaction Training Program up to this point, you have probably developed a great deal of inner confidence about expressing your sexual desires. You have also shown your partner that fulfilling your desires has big benefits for him, too. All you need to do now is pick a quiet time (perhaps after sex) and let your creative juices flow. Be sure to stop short of actual fantasy-sharing however; that is the massage oil that lubricates the next preliminary step.

If you do feel any residual awkwardness about expressing your erotic ideas, or if acting out your fantasies seems somehow more daunting to you than talking about them, don't let your inhibitions get in the way of your satisfaction. Use one of these alternative methods and make your lover an offer he can't refuse.

Write a Letter. Describe a fantasy you want to act out; be loving, but get right to the point. "Dear Honey: You've been in my thoughts again! As a result, there's a sexual fantasy I would like to try. . . ." Then describe the fantasy in full, from the enticing clothes you will wear to the delicious things you will do. Remember, however: play-acting is rooted in the physical world. Let your imagination wander, but tempt your lover with real activities you can consummate or simulate in the real world. If, for example, your sexual desire is to make love in a jungle surrounded by animals, tell your lover how you intend to authenticate the setting. ("We can play a record with jungle sound effects and turn up the heat so it's like making love in the equatorial zone.") Once you've put your ideas on paper, give the letter to your partner and wait for his response. You won't have long to wait.

Tape It. Describe your fantasy—and how you want to act it out—into a tape recorder, then let your partner listen in on your secret thoughts. This option spares you the discomfort of spilling your guts in a face-to-face confrontation. Feel free to *say* what's on your mind without self-censoring, the way you might if your partner were standing right in front of you. If you can, allow yourself to free associate into the recorder. Open up about the wildest things you want to do. Hearing your voice will make the experience more immediate for him. And put some oomph into it! A sexy, sultry tone conveys a very seductive message. But be genuine. When you're through, just give the tape to your partner—or leave it in his car with instructions that he play it on the way home from work. He'll get back to you in record time.

Make a Wish. Compose a Play-acting Wish List. Itemize all the fabulous fantasies you want to act out with your lover. Keep the descriptions brief, but flesh them out enough to give him some sense of what's in store. When you're finished with the list, allow your man to browse among your fantasies like a kid in a candy store. I guarantee, he'll be sweet on this idea.

Write Play-acting Want Ads. You won't send these to the newspaper; these saucy solicitations are strictly for home use. On separate index cards, write down each fantasy you would like to act out, in the form of a classified ad. For instance:

Wanted: Man who will be my private Chippendales dancer for an evening wearing only a bow tie and a smile. (Bow tie optional.)

Wanted: Man who will rub me down with flavored oil and have me for dessert.

Wanted: Man who will give me a champagne bubble bath, sprinkle me with rose petals, then make love to me on satin sheets all night long.

Leave these around the house where your partner is sure to find them: on his favorite easy chair, in front of the television, on his dresser, taped to the refrigerator door, on the bed, in the pocket of his coat, or scrawled in lipstick on the bathroom mirror. Keep track of which get "answered" first. If a certain ad works for you, you know it worked its magic on your lover. You can expand on it during the next play-acting session—or in the next want ad.

Send a Fantasy Greeting Card. Buy or make a blank greeting card with a sexy cover, describe your fantasy inside, then mail the card to your partner at home (or, if you want to live a little more dangerously, at work). Be creative with the return address if you like—bill yourself as "Candy Kane," or "Wicked Wanda," or "Naughty Nancy." Be sure not to include your real address if you do. Postal-service employees have fantasies of their own, you know.

Letting your partner in on your sexual secrets can be a real tease. Communicating your desires in surprising ways lets him know that the one thing he can always expect from you is the unexpected—and nothing is more exhilarating than a partner who keeps you on your toes!

But sometimes just telling him about the fantasy is

not enough. You may want to get to know it more intimately before you start acting it out. There is no better means to that end than . . .

Preliminary Step 3: Share Your Sexual Secrets During Lovemaking

At this point, you might be ready to jump into costume and jump into bed! If you are truly comfortable with your role and deeply knowledgeable about your fantasy, you might consider this an optional step and proceed with the role-play. But if you want to get a preview of how your play-acting debut might turn out, or if you have any trepidations at all about bringing your sexual dream to life, I suggest that you share the fantasy with your partner during lovemaking, using the fantasy-sharing technique in chapter 7.

Fantasy-sharing as a prelude to play-acting is like dipping your toe in the ocean before taking a swim. You may learn that the fantasy is lukewarm at best—amusing enough as a shared idea, but not worth the plunge as a full-scale production. You will also learn whether or not a fantasy is likely to take you in over your head or make you uncomfortable in any way—or whether you will be able to enjoy without reservation this refreshing dip into a new sexual dimension.

When you share the fantasy with your partner, do so with the idea in mind that your next step is to act it out. See how that makes you feel. If you have any concerns, reevaluate the scenario. You might decide to build on what you like about it and disregard the rest. Or you can choose another fantasy altogether. (Remember: in Wonderland, there's always more where that sexy daydream came from!)

Once you are satisfied that the fantasy will last as long as your passion, there is nothing holding you back. Set the scene, dim the lights, climb into your costume, and get on with the show!

Play-acting: How to Bring Your Fantasies to Life

You might be "a simple girl with a dream," but if head-to-toe sexual satisfaction is what you've been dreaming of, here is how to make your erotic wishes come true!

Step 1: Plan for Pleasure

If staging your fantasy requires anything other than you, your partner, and your naked bodies, now is the time to organize the costumes, accessories, mirrors, music, videotaping equipment, love oils, or any sexual props you will need to make your fantasy real.

Nothing ties up an otherwise smooth scenario like digging through a cluttered scarf drawer so you can tie your partner to the bed. And nothing keeps the excitement from building like a construction worker who can't locate his tool! It's your party—so plan it like one! Have a brainstorming session with your lover about what it will take to make this happening happen—then get your massagers in a row so neither of you comes up empty-handed at a crucial moment.

Of course, if you want to surprise your partner, you will need to keep the planning process under your hat—or, in the case of one woman I know, under your leather headband. One dreary Saturday, she decorated her entire bedroom in a sixties theme: beaded curtains in the doorway, a black light on the dresser, psychedelic posters on the wall, patchouli incense burning on a table, and Jimi Hendrix playing in the background. She met her husband at the door wearing a headband, a tie-dyed T-shirt, and bell-bottom jeans that were teasingly unbuttoned (no panties underneath). The scenario took them both back to their school days in the age of free love. It took thirty years off their sex lives—and added immeasurably to their relationship.

If your fantasy has to do with a specific sexual act rather than a minidrama, now is the time to gather everything you need to make that activity happen in safe, comfortable surroundings. Pile soft pillows on the floor to cushion your entrée into a new form of sex. Stash any lubricants, sex toys, or accessories within easy reach. If you'll be using condoms, buy some in neon colors—just for fun. You never know when you'll have to find something important in the dark.

Step 2: Dress the Part

No two ways about it: in play-acting putting your desires into action is the main event, but dressing the part is a deliciously exciting form of foreplay. Whether you'll be wearing a G-string or the height of drop-dead glamour, this is the moment when you transform yourself into the real-life personification of your secret desires. And whether your lover is swathed in a silk robe or arrayed in full battle dress, he will know that he is a short march away from the place where reality ends and the world of your erotic dreams begins.

You may dress in front of each other; you may decide to actually dress each other; or you may choose to repair to private quarters and spring your new looks on

each other as a surprise—whatever sets the mood.
When you are ready, put on some music that enhances
the scene. Then take a moment or two to get physically
and emotionally comfortable in your clothes—and in
your new roles.

As stimulated as you may be, don't press for immediate action. Set your mind on what you will be doing,
focus on how you intend to channel your fantasy
through the character you will be playing, and, most of
all, *relax*. Remember: this is not an audition. Your partner has already selected you as the liberator of his secret sexual fantasies, as well as the love of his life. The
only task before you now is to achieve a state of total
relaxation so you can move naturally through the phases of your fantasy, follow the dictates of your desires,
and take all the pleasure that comes your way in the
process. When you are able to focus on your feelings
without any distractions, when you feel that you have
really become your character (and are no longer worried if your costume is becoming to you), the time is
right. You can begin to put your needs into action.

Step 3: Action!

Find a starting point that feels comfortable within
the atmosphere you have created, then allow your character to reveal herself as naturally as possible. If, for
example, you and your lover are at a nightclub pretending to be strangers, size him up as if you were inspecting
a prime cut of beef. Intrigue him with some subtle teasing. Drop your napkin; look down at it and then back
up at him suggestively. Hesitate. Then bend down and
show him some of your thigh as you pick it up. Or strut
past the length of the bar stroking the counter with

one languid finger as you do. Don't make it easy for yourselves to bring the fantasy to its climax; draw out the sexual tension and delay immediate gratification, knowing it will bring greater pleasure later.

If you find it awkward to get started (a little stage fright is to be expected when one is making her play-acting debut!), make your intentions plain. State your business as simply and provocatively as possible. If you are playing a doctor and your partner is the patient, break the ice by saying something like, "I'm going to begin the examination by taking your blood pressure, so why don't you lie down while I find the best place to take a good, strong pulse." Your partner won't take his role lying down for long. Once he responds, the minidrama will be off and running at a fever pitch.

It takes two to play-act. Unless your partner is actively involved in developing his character and playing his role, the plot will become one-sided, stilted, and, ultimately, unsatisfying. If your man-of-few-words has willingly dressed the part, take heart: he has already shown you that he is willing to participate in the fulfillment of your fantasy. He may be waiting for direction from you. Or he may simply be hanging on to your every word with bated breath, wondering what new plot twist you'll come up with next. If you need to, draw him out with the techniques I suggested on page 123. Once he gets over his uncertainty, momentum (and his own need for sexual release) will take over.

Step 4: Let Your Feelings Go

Because play-acting makes your wildest fantasies real, it is the ultimate body-mind connection. Needless to say, you will probably experience some very strong sexual feelings as your secret desires take on a life of their own. If there ever was an appropriate time to lie back and enjoy it, this is it! Let your feelings go. Allow yourself to be swept away by the current as your desires rush to pleasure. You will probably find yourself using strong, sexy language you would never otherwise use. Turn the air blue! Get it out of your system. If you are shocked by what you hear yourself saying, remind yourself that a real feeling lies behind every fantasy and that, with the exception of anger, your feelings are better out than in during this scenario. If anger comes up for you, that's fine, but try not to deal with it when you're in the middle of making love. Anger is a strong emotion that always inhibits your ability to enjoy yourself. So stop the game and work through the feeling, asking for your partner's help; otherwise it could lead to a negative experience for both of you.

Other than acting on anger or physically hurting your partner, any activity that heightens your excitement and moves the plot along is fair game. If, for example, you are experimenting with the pleasures of anal penetration and it's turning you on, you can immerse yourself in the pleasure of the moment—or develop a character through which you can express different attitudes about this variation. You may pretend that your lover is in a position of power while he is thrusting in you. You may imagine that you are the object of his sexual obsession. You may even "tussle" with him, or pretend that you are trying to escape his grasp. Whatever sexual activity you choose, experiment with what you are doing. Use your new roles as a reason to seek pleasure in new ways. And always let your feelings—not repressive social taboos—be your guide.

Step 5: Let the Plot Develop

Scripting your game of let's pretend is a truly collab-orative venture. Once you and your partner get your creative juices flowing, you will find that one erotic idea invariably leads to another, and another, and an-other . . . until you find yourself acting out unimagin-able unique variations, all branching from the same initial fantasy.

Go with the flow! Suppose your initial desire was to incorporate food into your lovemaking. Let's say you began by sitting on your partner's lap and feeding him sensually. He may have decided to give you a taste of your own fantasy by covering his vegetables in dip, rub-bing it onto your nipples, and licking it off. Before you know it, you may find yourself making love on the kitchen table or out on the deck, pouring champagne all over yourself and your partner. What began as a sim-ple idea has evolved into a progressive love feast—with more taste treats to come.

But themes are not laws, and laying them down as if they were can keep you from exploring your fantasy in all its depth. Suppose, in your erotic dream, you and your lover are artists who are inspired to make living masterpieces of each other with colorful, edible body paints. A few strokes here, a few licks there, and tech-nically you're done. But if you get into the sensuality of the experience, if you allow your creativity to flow as freely as the paint, your sensual artistry may take a dif-ferent shape altogether. You may be inspired to enact roles that correspond to the designs you've painted on your bodies (*Anything-but-Still Life on Top of a Piano* perhaps?). Or you may decide to sport your renderings like underclothes: get dressed up and go out to dinner, knowing all the while that under your formal attire you are both painted up like billboards. Finally, you can cap the evening off by going to a drive-in movie, tearing each other's clothes off in the back seat, devouring the edible paints, and writing suggestive messages to each other in the car windows you've steamed up.

The script of your fantasy may be the foundation upon which your excitement builds, but the dramatic embellishments you add in the throes of passion are the architectural details that make the structure of your relationship come alive! Be spontaneous. Take risks. Allow your sexual fantasies to fulfill themselves and *you* will be fulfilled—as a creator, as a lover, and as a sexually satisfied woman.

The Limitless Pleasures of Play-acting. Sometimes you will use up a fantasy in a single lovemaking session; sometimes the role you have chosen will leave you wanting more. Often, it will seem that you have exhausted a fantasy—only to have a deeper, more intriguing one spring up in its place. In any case, there are more than enough erotic scenarios and sensual variations available to you courtesy of your Wonderland to give your adventure in play-acting a limitless run. Here are some ways to take this technique further.

- Build on an exciting aspect of your fantasy that you didn't expand fully in the previous session. If you dressed up in costumes and pretended to be characters in a minidrama, make the costumes more titillating, or develop the characters in a more interesting way.

- Act out a totally new fantasy. Dip into your "wish list" or, for a real change of pace, ask your partner to write *his* fantasies on slips of paper, put them in a hat, then act out the one you pull out together.

- Try acting out a fantasy you've read or heard about. See what it's like to try someone else's fantasy on for size. You may plug into an electrifying scenario that you never would have dreamed up yourself.

- Alternate between play-acting and fantasy-sharing. One night, talk your sexual secrets out for your pleasure and your partner's; several nights later, bring an entirely new fantasy to life in all its glory. Or mix the two activities. Use fantasy-sharing to "test drive" a fantasy you want to act out or as "afterplay" to a fantasy you've already acted out. If you're really feeling like the Sarah Bernhardt of the boudoir, you might even try verbally sharing one fantasy while acting out another.

QUESTIONS AND ANSWERS
ABOUT PLAY-ACTING

Play-acting and fantasy-sharing tap into the same source—your Wonderland—but the result can be very different. While in fantasy-sharing you painted a verbal portrait of your desires, play-acting allows your sexual secrets to take shape in a physical, tangible way. As your fantasies take on a real dimension, your inhibitions, fears, and concerns may become more real, too.

You will notice that some of the following questions

are the same as those in chapter 7. Fantasy-sharing and
play-acting are commonly misunderstood but uniquely
different techniques. By applying the same questions to
each subject, I hope to underscore the relevant differ-
ences between these powerful and transformational sexual variations. To further deepen your understanding, I
have also included three new questions that are specific
to play-acting.

*What if I have a sexual fantasy about another man, such as
a movie star, or a stranger, or a friend? Should I act it out
with my partner? Is it unfair or disloyal to ask my lover to
play the role of the other man?*

If the man in your erotic dreams is inaccessible (a
movie star, a man you saw once and will never see
again, or the idealized, faceless stranger who stars in so
many fantasies), and your partner is game, by all means
ask him to help you live out the fantasy. Scenarios like
these are totally harmless, but if you do them up right
(with the appropriate costumes, impersonation, and
whatever other tricks you'd like to come up with) they
can be tremendously fun and fulfilling for you and your
lover.

If, however, the man in your fantasy is an accessible
man—a neighbor, your partner's best friend, a coworker,
your best girlfriend's husband, or even the repairman—I
advise you *not* to bring this fantasy to life. It can be very
exciting to simulate making love with a man you know.
If the play-acting is stimulating and satisfying for you, you
may begin to associate the real erotic validation you got
from the role-play with the real person in your fantasy.
One look from him may be all it takes to rekindle those

urges in you. The next thing you know, your interest in your marriage is in jeopardy.

I repeat: fantasizing about a personal friend or a family acquaintance is *not* the way to maintain fidelity. I urge you *not* to act the fantasy out but to talk it out with your partner or in a counseling setting.

What if my partner thinks I'm strange, or weird, because of one of my fantasies?

There's a great quote on fantasies and it goes like this: "An improper mind is a perpetual feast." If your lover has been feasting sexually on your desires, he is not likely to complain about the exotic nature of the tasty fantasies you've been piling on his plate.

If he does balk at a specific scenario, however, don't let his hesitancy get in the way of your fulfillment. Talk the fantasy out, get to the root of his discomfort, and try to arrive at a workable compromise between the satisfaction you want and the pleasure your partner is capable of giving. If your fantasy is a strong, persistent one and your partner is able to meet you halfway on it, without judging you, that may be enough to put the erotic dream to rest. But if your partner continues to view you as "different," or if he will not yield on a fantasy you have a very strong need to express, then you have to evaluate the direction of your partnership. Will it give you the intimate fulfillment you seek for the future? Or is your continued repression a prerequisite for your partner's happiness—sexual or otherwise?

Erotic fantasies are usually not strong enough to make or break a marriage, but your ongoing sexual satisfaction can make a huge difference in the health and longevity of your relationship. If your partner's attitude reflects an inability to trust you, a fundamental difference in your sexual natures, or a serious rift in intimacy, then your marriage or relationship may be in trouble. In that case, you should seek counseling.

What if I become obsessed with a fantasy and keep thinking about it over and over again?

You just bought a new CD you've been wanting and for two weeks straight you play it over and over. Is that an obsession? No, it's enjoyment! And so it is with your sexual fantasies.

Some erotic dreams are one-shot wonders. They burst into your mind, blaze briefly, and are exhausted quickly. But others are as fresh and exciting the hundredth time you enact them as they were the first. Why not go for an encore performance? The worst thing that could happen is that, during the 101st revival, the fantasy would lose its erotic edge. The most likely thing that would happen is that you and your partner would have a rip-roaring time.

Of course, if you can't seem to get a fantasy out of your mind and you don't *want* it there, you may need to seek some assistance—but not before you try expressing your desires, through play-acting or fantasy-sharing.

Fantasies don't progress in a linear way, as do the minutes, hours, and years of our lives. Stop a fantasy at any point, take a look around you, and you will be treated to a virtual panorama of possibilities. One scenario can go in literally hundreds of directions—all stemming from one path.

So don't confuse your own creativity with addiction.

It's hard to become truly addicted to a fantasy, unless some underlying need in you is not being fulfilled. If that is the case, express as much as you can of the fantasy, and if it still bothers you, seek outside help.

I'm afraid that if I try play-acting I'll lose control and wind up doing strange things sexually. Can such a thing happen?

If you are sexually active, you are already doing things sexually. If play-acting is new and strange to you, it is understandable that you might make the mental leap from "doing things sexually" to "doing *strange* things sexually."

Play-acting is a uniquely liberating experience. At its best, it is the triumph of freedom over inhibition, over societal repression, even over the pressure to "be yourself." That said, it is not unlikely that—in the throes of passion—you will find yourself doing something that seems out of character—spewing epithets that would never cross your tongue in daily life, or initiating activities you would never admit, in polite conversation, to finding appealing. Let me put it another way. If someone taking a survey phoned you at home and asked, "Would you ever make love with your partner in the mud on a dismal, rainy day?" you would probably answer, "No way! What a gross idea!" Yet, the next evening, you might find yourself rained in in a romantic cabin in the mountains. If you and your partner ran out to get some wood for the fireplace, became invigorated by the rain, chased each other through the woods, and, after a short wrestle on the ground, made passionate love right there in the mud, would that be strange? Yes. It would be out of the context of your sexual routine. Would it be gross? Hardly. It would be memorable.

The great psychologist Sigmund Freud said that we human beings retain much of our animal natures, even though we are no longer animals. If that's so, it's not strange to get in touch with the animal in you during an activity as elemental as sex. In fact, some of the best sex happens when there is a jungle beat in the background and you are the animal of your dreams. So don't be afraid to explore play-acting and all it has to offer. You might momentarily lose control, but you'll be compensated for your loss a thousand times over.

Is there a chance that things could go too far during a play-acting game and either I or my partner could get hurt?

Getting hurt is a fear similar to the fear of losing control. Therefore, it is a common fear among those who dabble in the more daring and adventurous forms of play-acting, such as bondage, playful spanking, or discipline.

But going too far is not limited to role-playing. Couples often cross the line between pain and pleasure in the course of regular, everyday sex. In the heat of passion, a woman may dig her nails a little too forcefully into her partner's back. A man may playfully wrestle his lover and hurt her.

The real fear underlying this question is that something that comes up during play-acting will spark anger: that your partner will lose control and get rough with you—or you will get rough with him. This is a fear of the unknown—a nagging doubt about what lies hidden in your partner and in yourself.

As you already know, behind almost every fantasy

is a feeling. If you know your partner—and yourself—well enough, you have a sense of what kinds of feelings he—and you—are harboring. You also have a sense of whether either of you is capable of getting out of hand physically. To put your mind at ease, I suggest you talk out your fears with your partner before attempting any play-acting experience. Come right out and say what you're afraid of, no matter how irrational it might sound to you: "Honey, I want to try this game, but I'm afraid you might get carried away and hurt me. I don't want to be hurt. What do you feel about this? Can I trust you to be gentle with me?" Then give your partner a chance to air his thoughts. You may discover that he has fears, too. If he does, let him express them, and respond to them honestly. Trust is a critical component in achieving sexual satisfaction. Talk things out until you feel comfortable putting your fantasy—and your physical safety—in your partner's hands.

For further reassurance, you can also set limits for any game of let's pretend. Be clear about which activities you will tolerate and which you won't. Make an agreement with your lover that he will stop the game and talk about any feeling that comes up that could lead to a negative experience—and that you will do the same. Designate a code word or phrase that, when spoken by one of you, will signal to the other that the game is to be stopped immediately, say, "stop!," "time out!," "hold it," "that's enough," or "uncle." Whatever word you choose, make sure it is one that you or your partner can't possibly confuse as being part of the game.

To give yourself an extra measure of security, leave yourself an out if a planned activity involves a feeling

of helplessness on your part. For example, if you are going to let your partner tie you to the bed, have him tie
the scarves snugly enough so you have the sensation of
helplessness but loosely enough so you can escape at
any time. Don't put yourself in a position where you
can experience a sense of panic, claustrophobia, or
powerlessness.

If you're still vacillating between intrigue and fear
about a specific scenario, act out the minidrama with
your respective roles reversed. Tie *him* up first, if that's
what you ultimately want to have done to you. Then
discuss how he felt during the game. His revelations
may give you a preview of the kinds of feelings you will
experience when you switch roles. You may also learn
whether your fears are justified or not.

Finally, if you are in a casual relationship with your
partner, such as a "friends and sex" affair, I advise you
to stay away from any play-acting games that require
you to entrust your physical well-being to a partner you
don't really know. True sexual satisfaction can only be
achieved in comfortable, safe relationships, those firmly
rooted in mutual respect. And, needless to say, safe sex
is something I'm behind 100 percent.

Are there any fantasies I should NOT *act out?*

Since physical pain is a sure sign of damage to the
body, and emotional pain is not productive in any
sexual milieu, I do not recommend acting out any
fantasy that hurts—physically or emotionally.

Playful scolding is provocative. ("You've been bad
today, and I'm going to have to teach you a lesson
you'll never forget.") But verbal abuse is unpleasant
and always destructive. Such harsh exchanges have

no place in the bedroom—and no place in a loving relationship. In other words, if it feels good, do it! If it doesn't, don't.

Won't acting out my fantasy ruin the erotic scenario in my mind? Aren't fantasies richer in my imagination than they could ever be in reality?

It is possible that enacting your favorite fantasy won't live up to your dreams. But it's more probable that your erotic ideas will be bigger and better in reality than they ever were in your imagination.

A fantasy shared is not a fantasy halved—it is a fantasy doubled! To understand how this works (and in keeping with the mathematical metaphor), you need only remember this ratio: a private fantasy is to a shared fantasy what masturbation is to lovemaking. As solitary, one-dimensional pursuits, masturbation and private fantasies go hand in hand to provide you with limited and superficial comfort and release. While these activities may suit your immediate needs, they will never approximate the deep satisfaction you get from lovemaking with a caring partner. The point is clear: alone with your dreams, you will never achieve the physical and emotional one–two punch you get from sharing or enacting them with your lover.

Nor will you ever "ruin" or diminish a vivid fantasy by bringing it to life. Your mind does not work like a tin can. Once opened, its contents do not spill out. A favorite fantasy, then, will always remain in your mind, growing and developing as props, costumes, and scenes are added to it. Even if you act out that fantasy with less than riveting results, the erotic scenario itself is not diminished. It still exists, unchanged, in your Wonderland. You can return to it—or any variation of it—any time you like.

So when can an erotic idea be more potent than reality? When your real partner does not measure up to the idealized man in your fantasy. If, for example, you have been dreaming of a roll in the hay with an incredibly muscular farmhand and you are married to Mr. Peepers, you are bound to be disappointed by the inappropriate stand-in. Or if, like many women, you have entertained the fantasy of intercourse with a remarkably well-endowed stranger, you can expect your average-sized partner to fall short of the role.

Although this kind of real-body-to-idealized-body comparison is unfair (how would you feel if your partner let you know that you didn't measure up to his physical ideal?), some of these details—like penis size— can be simulated. But the best news is, they probably won't have to be. By virtue of this program, you have made your partner into the lover of your dreams. The powerful combination of his lovemaking skills and your sexual liberation are a more than equal match to any scenario that exists in your mind. And when it comes to putting that kind of passion into motion, "ain't nothin' like the real thing, baby!"

Your quest for sexual satisfaction is a powerful and primal example of the natural life force at work. Your sexual fantasies not only stimulate, shape, and define that quest, they ultimately fulfill it.

This exploration of the pleasures of play-acting may mark the end of the Five-Step Program, but it does not mark the end of your journey to sexual satisfaction. The Well of Sexual Dreams never runs dry. Sustained by an endless source of erotic refreshment, you will go on discovering the virgin territory of your sexuality forever.

Will you and your partner become the Lewis and Clark of erotic exploration? That has been the happy destiny of countless couples, including Donna and Bill, who tell their frustration-to-fulfillment story in the pages to come.

9 ～

Donna: Case History of a Satisfied Woman

～

Although Donna is not her real name, this is the real-life sexual success story of a thirty-eight-year-old woman who—through my Five-Step Program—is now getting everything she wants from her husband, in bed and out!

When Donna first came to see me, she had been married to Bill, forty-two, for sixteen years. They had a fourteen-year-old daughter, a committed relationship, and, as Donna described it, a sex life that was going nowhere. In fact, only minutes into our first meeting Donna began to relate a virtual roll call of problems plaguing her sex life with Bill:

- When she and Bill had sex, there was very little foreplay. Intercourse was always a "slam, bam, thank you, ma'am" affair that left Donna frustrated.

- While having sex with Bill, Donna would often wonder, Maybe he'll try something new this time. Maybe he'll surprise me, rather than doing it the same old way. Though nothing extraordinary ever happened between the sheets, Donna waited passively for years, hoping things would get better.

- Bill never talked during sex. Donna had all kinds of things she wanted to say—all kinds of fantasies she wanted to talk about—but since Bill was always so quiet, she never felt open about expressing her feelings. She was embarrassed to talk during sex because she felt Bill would not respond.

- Because sex was so dull with Bill, Donna's mind would tend to wander to other things—maybe chores she had to do, or sexual fantasies about other men.

- Pushed to the limit, Donna finally decided to take action. She began to suggest different positions to Bill, made herself available in different rooms of the house, and created a romantic atmosphere before sex. But to no avail. Sex for Bill always seemed to have a five-minute limit.

Donna also revealed that her sexual dissatisfaction was inspiring intensely graphic sexual fantasies about other men—during the day, when she was at work, and at night, when she was having sex with Bill. The sight of a man's derriere was enough to turn Donna on—and provide her with enough sexual daydreams to last her all day long. Several times, she indulged her fantasies by going to a male strip show with her friends. Of course, she became very aroused watching the men dance, and she always left the club with a headful of wildly erotic ideas. But when she went home and saw Bill, her arousal was eclipsed by a nagging sense of disappointment. Her husband just didn't measure up to those bumping, grinding, titillating dancers. And although the "hot topic" of the strip show, if shared in bed, would have made for great sex between her and Bill, she always kept her fantasies to herself. For one thing, she was embarrassed to admit that she *had* fantasies. Donna also felt that Bill would feel inadequate if he knew that she had been aroused by younger, sexier men.

In light of her active fantasy life and her boredom in the bedroom with Bill, it didn't surprise me to learn that Donna turned to her vibrator for sexual release. In fact, she masturbated so frequently that she gave her vibrator a pet name: "Charlie." When it eventually broke down, she immediately replaced it with a new one: "Dick."

Donna's revelations seemed to spill out before she could censor them—and she was clearly disconcerted by having aired her sexual laundry to me. When I reassured her that it was not unusual for couples to reach this point of stagnation, she was immediately relieved. And when I told her that breaking the chain of frustration could actually be fun, she was eager to begin. Right then and there, we set the program in motion by outlining the basic sexual desires she wanted Bill to fulfill—but didn't have the courage to express:

- She wanted Bill to engage in more foreplay with her during sex rather than rushing to the "main event."

- She wanted Bill to take their sex life off the clock: she wanted him to try to last longer in bed and not consider the encounter finished when he was finished.

- She wanted Bill to develop more rhythm during their lovemaking, to move a little more fluidly and use his body in a sexy (rather than rigid) way.

- She wanted their lovemaking to be more spontaneous and spur of the moment.

- She wanted Bill to treat her tenderly in bed—to touch her with sensitivity both emotionally and physically.

- She also wanted Bill to be rough and overpowering in bed on occasion, but in a way that was erotically stimulating to her—not just to please himself.

With all the erotic fantasies dancing in her head, Donna's Well of Sexual Dreams was clearly overflowing! It didn't take her long to enumerate some of the richly creative sensual scenarios she wanted to explore with Bill:

- She had fantasies of walking outside dressed in a sexy miniskirt, with no panties or bra on, and bending over for Bill and other men to see. In a related fantasy, she would go to the beach dressed in a string bikini and strut her stuff in front of all the men.

- She imagined what it would be like to be a stripper at a night club—to get up on stage and take it all off, piece by tantalizing piece, in front of an audience of men—including Bill. In her erotic scenario, her dance was accompanied by sexy music, enhanced by flashing lights, and visible from all angles in mirrors surrounding the stage. In her fantasy, she continued the tease until she had given all the men erections.

- She had a fantasy of picking up a handsome stranger, then "getting to know him" on her living room floor.

- She fantasized being a high-class call girl who would have sex with any good-looking man who could pay her premium prices. Donna wanted to dress up like a prostitute one night and make Bill pay to have sex with her.

- She imagined having sex with two men at the same time—either Bill and a stranger, or Bill and someone she knew. This led to a fantasy about wanting to have ten men make love to her at once. She dreamed of going to the stadium locker room of her city's professional football team and having sex with everyone on the team.

- She fantasized being tied to the bed and held as a sexual captive by Bill or a stranger. She also had the desire to blindfold Bill, tie *him* to the bed— then drive him crazy with pleasure.

Like you, Donna began the program by giving Bill the LoveSkills Makeover. Once she taught Bill how to touch her and where to touch her, she used her ingenuity to reinforce what he had learned—in the most mutually pleasurable way possible. She bought some body paints (the edible kind) and turned herself into an erotic "road map" of what she wanted in bed. Arrows pointed to where she wanted to be touched; "road signs" explained, in the most graphic language, how to handle each of her "dangerous curves." She even included lighthearted warnings such as CAUTION: Road Narrows to make Bill do what he had never done before in bed—laugh.

When Donna learned the PowerTease Method, as presented in chapter 5, she really cut loose! The suggested teases not only fit right in with Donna's fantasies, they ignited an erotic renaissance of creative ideas she could use to turn Bill on so he would do virtually anything she wanted in bed:

- She cooked in the nude, or served dinner wearing only an apron.

- When Donna and Bill were out horseback riding in a secluded area, she took off her shirt and rode topless. The wind made her nipples erect—and Bill spent more time looking at her breasts than at the scenery.

- She wrote on her breasts with Day-Glo-colored body paint. When Bill exposed them, they instructed him to KISS THESE.

- She bought some stick-on tattoos (the kind that wash off easily), then arranged them on her body to form a pictorial menu of what Bill could expect for the evening. For example, she applied a tattoo of a unicorn with the horn between her breasts, to suggest a new activity they could engage in.

- She had sexy photos taken of herself by a boudoir photographer. She surprised Bill by mailing them to him—at work.

- She went to a special erotic baker and had a cake made of a woman's naked body. As Bill ate it for dessert, she made appropriate erotic suggestions.

- Donna wanted to get Bill to go to the gym and exercise. So she said to him one day, "Why don't you come down to the gym and see what I do in my aerobics class?" He said, "I don't want to go to the gym. Why don't you just show me your routine?" Of course, the sexy aerobics strip that followed was anything but routine. Now they go to the gym together. At workout time, Donna always takes a spot in front of Bill so he can watch her exercise her option for seduction.

- Every once in a while, Donna intentionally lets two, three, even four days pass without having sex with Bill. During that time, she does her best to turn him on. She combs her hair while topless, for example, wearing only a pair of pants. She pulls on her stockings slowly, then attaches them to a sexy garter belt. Or she works out on their exercise machine in the nude. Finally, when they can't stand it anymore, she allows Bill to touch her— and they enjoy the kind of no-holds-barred sex that's worth waiting for.

Wild Nights . . . and Days. The Wild Night experience turned out to be one of the most exciting and transformational parts of the training program for Donna. Since Bill was by now totally enchanted by his newly liberated sex life, Donna got to try out several of the vignettes I presented in chapter 6. But she did me one better—and nearly did Bill in!—when she came up with her own Wild Night scenario. It went like this:

One day, Donna came upon a box of memorabilia she and Bill had accumulated throughout their years together. In the box she found Bill's copy of their college yearbook, and tucked inside were letters and photos from an old romance with a girl named Anne.

Donna didn't tell Bill of her find. But sure enough, several days later Bill got a blast from the past. While he was at work, he was hand-delivered a mysterious envelope. Inside was a hotel room key and a note with a typed message: "I'm a friend of yours from the past. If you still have that marvelous sense of adventure I remember so well, just come to my room and open the door. Meanwhile, let me give you some clues about who I am. . . ." The rest of the letter painted a picture of a woman who was remarkably similar to Anne.

Bill suspected that this was Donna's doing, but he couldn't be sure. He also wasn't sure whether to take the mystery woman up on her challenge. If it was Donna, this would be an exciting liaison. If it wasn't, the meeting might be too hot to handle. Either way, he decided to call his pen pal's bluff.

After work, Bill hightailed it to the hotel, found the room, and opened the door. Inside, he found himself in a luxurious suite with a huge bathtub in the center. Water had been drawn and the tub was overflowing with bubbles. Around it, flickering candles provided the only illumination in the room.

Bill's eyes were still adjusting to the low light when

a woman appeared from the bedroom. At first, Bill
didn't recognize her. Donna was a brunette, but this
woman had shoulder-length auburn hair. Unlike Donna, she wore lots of makeup—and a long silk robe Bill
had never seen before. Bill was honestly confused. He
began to stammer out an apology. Only when the
woman approached, only when she allowed the robe to
part teasingly to give Bill a glimpse of the black lingerie
she wore underneath, was Bill sure that the mystery
woman was Donna. He moved to embrace her, but she
kept him at arm's length. Then she said, "We can continue the game but under one condition: *I* get to do
what I want tonight."

Bill agreed without one ounce of protest. It was a
night they would both remember—he because it was
such a pleasant surprise, and Donna because she got to
realize many unfulfilled sexual fantasies.

As Donna began to feel more comfortable with her
sexuality, she began to share her most intimate
thoughts with Bill while they made love, using the
fantasy-sharing techniques presented in chapter 7.
When Donna revealed that she had fantasies that included other men, Bill was upset at first. But once he
realized that fantasies were *ideas,* and ideas posed no
threat to his masculinity or his marriage, he felt secure
enough to take pleasure from Donna's pleasure. Not
only did Bill enjoy his trips to Donna's Wonderland, he
even helped her simulate some of her wildest scenarios.
For instance, he simultaneously stimulated her with a
vibrator and his mouth to indulge her desire to be plea-
sured by two men.

Donna reached the pinnacle of her sexuality when
she got to the play-acting portion of the program. Using the techniques in chapter 8, she acted out many of

the fantasies she had revealed to Bill during the fantasy-sharing part of the program. And because the Well of Sexual Dreams is a "hot spring" that never runs dry, she came up with enough scenarios and sexual Varieties to outdo Baskin-Robbins:

- She dressed up in a candy striper outfit one night and "nursed" Bill back to sexual health.

- She dressed up as a high-class call girl and made Bill pay for her "services."

- She created a costume for every phase of their relationship and marriage—their first date, their courtship, their honeymoon, their second honeymoon ten years later, etc. She wore these outfits on successive nights while she and her husband relived their history (and made some!) in bed.

- She took a bottle of Kahlua into the bedroom one night, poured it all over her naked body, and had Bill lick it off.

- She bought some edible underwear for Bill at an erotic-toy party—then ate the evidence.

- Late one night she went with Bill to an all-night supermarket wearing only a raincoat. When she exposed herself to him in the frozen foods aisle, she nearly caused a major thaw.

- She got Bill to make love to her while they were horseback riding in the back country. They sat naked, facing each other, on the horse and used the natural rhythm of the horse's motions to bring them both to a climax.

- They played Good Vibrations: she had Bill sit naked on his motorcycle while the engine idled in neutral. She then took her clothes off and sat on his lap, facing away from him and supporting herself with the handlebars. She had control of the throttle, and by turning the handle she would rev the engine a little bit to increase the vibrations. She reached several climaxes from the vibrations alone.

- One day she and Bill drove to a lake in the mountains. They rented inner tubes and floated to a remote area. When they were sure no one was around, they took off their bathing suits and floated around in the nude. At Donna's suggestion, they got into the same inner tube and made love.

- They saved up for a vacation to Jamaica. Late one night, after an evening on the town, Donna began climbing all over Bill in an elevator in their hotel. She asked the elevator operator to put the elevator on hold and take a break for awhile (and gave him a nice tip), then she and Bill made love on the elevator floor.

- One afternoon, Donna and Bill were house-hunting. While in one model home, she took Bill into a downstairs bathroom with no door on it and said, "Let's make love." They tried out the bathtub, vanity, and even the wall. Fortunately, no one came into the house during their tryst—but the thought of being discovered added lots of excitement to the experience.

- Donna had a fantasy about being spanked. One night while making love to Bill, she tried discreetly to get the message across. "Bill," she said, "I've been real naughty today. I didn't make you what you wanted for dinner, and I didn't get you your newspaper when you wanted it." Bill sensed what she was after, but he decided to tease her a little bit by pretending he didn't know what she was talking about. "That's okay, honey," he reassured her. "None of those details are important now."

   Donna was wise to him, but played along: "But you asked me to do just those few things for you. Don't you think it was naughty of me to ignore your needs?" "Honey, it's okay," soothed Bill. "Look, it happened—I'm sure you had a busy day."

   Finally, pretending to be frustrated, Donna took a cloth belt from her closet and began spanking herself with it. She said, "Don't you see, Bill? I've *really* been naughty!" Excited now, Bill gave in and "caught on." "Oh, I get it!" he said, taking the cloth belt from her. "You're right—you *are* a bad girl, Donna!"

- One night while they were making love, Donna got Bill to tie her to the bed with scarves and stockings and pretend he was taking advantage of her. It turned out to be one of the most exciting sexual experiences she ever had. Nothing passed between them that wasn't gentle and loving. Still, the sense that Donna was under Bill's control drove her wild, and the anticipation she felt—not knowing how Bill would choose to tease her next—was electric. The experience was the ulti-

mate realization of one of her deepest fantasies—
and it brought her almost more pleasure than she
could bear.

As for Bill, the encounter opened a whole new
dimension in sexual gratification. Making his wife
a prisoner to his loving hands, mouth and body,
watching her writhe under his touch, helpless to
escape, aroused him to the core. It also awakened
a fantasy for Bill: to make himself Donna's captive
of love.

Just a few weeks after beginning the program, Donna's sexuality began to blossom. Within months, the
methods she had learned had become a natural and liberating mode of erotic expression—and an integral part
of her personality. Released from her passivity, sexual
fire burned within her. She was able to express completely her passion, not in a rehearsed or forced way,
but as an indomitable lust for life, organic to her being.
In time, her whole demeanor took on a confident sensuality that was evident to everyone who saw her. She
had good reason to be confident. She had become
adept at teasing Bill in a way that was pleasurable to
both of them. She was able to challenge the man she
loved with her sexual needs without diminishing his
masculinity. And Donna had overcome her inhibitions.
Guided by the principles in this book, she had set herself free to explore every aspect of her sexuality. Having
cast aside guilt, shame, and embarrassment, she was left
with only joy and a free-flowing sense of adventure that
carried over into every aspect of her life.

In short, Donna had become a sexually satisfied
woman and, in the process, infused her marriage with

renewed strength, increased resilience, and a real chance at "happily ever after."

If you haven't done so before, I suggest that you re-take the Sexual Satisfaction Quiz now to chart the progress you've made along the way to your happy ending. I am confident that the results will confirm what you already know: that your inhibitions, passivity, and frustrations have become a thing of the past; that a lifetime of boundless adventure and limitless pleasure lies ahead, waiting to be discovered.

As you continue your exploration, I hope you will return to this book often for support, knowledge, and erotic inspiration. Much of the guidance within these pages has been provided by my clients and seminar attendees who, through this program, have successfully liberated their sexuality. I know that their stories and suggestions will speed your progress in discovering the sexually satisfied woman within you.

May all your erotic dreams come true!

AUTHOR'S NOTE
~

Dr. Ronnie Edell's research into the sexual issues that concern today's couples is an ongoing process. To this end, he welcomes input from his readers. If you have had any fantasies or experiences with this program you would like to share, of if you have comments, questions, or suggestions that may be addressed in a follow-up book, you may write to Dr. Edell at:

Dr. Ronnie Edell
P.O. Box 3718
La Mesa, CA 91944-3718